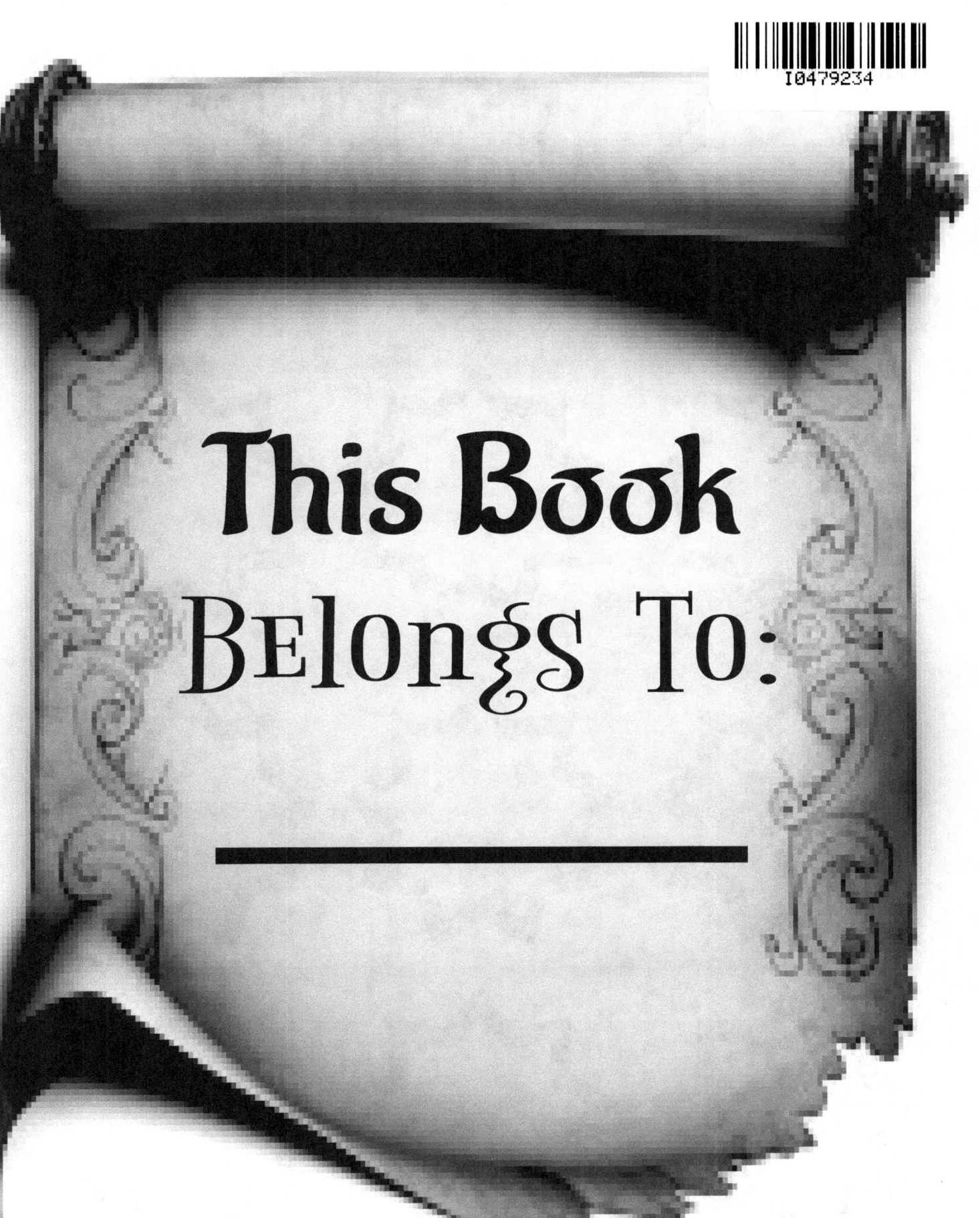

This Book Belongs To:

_____

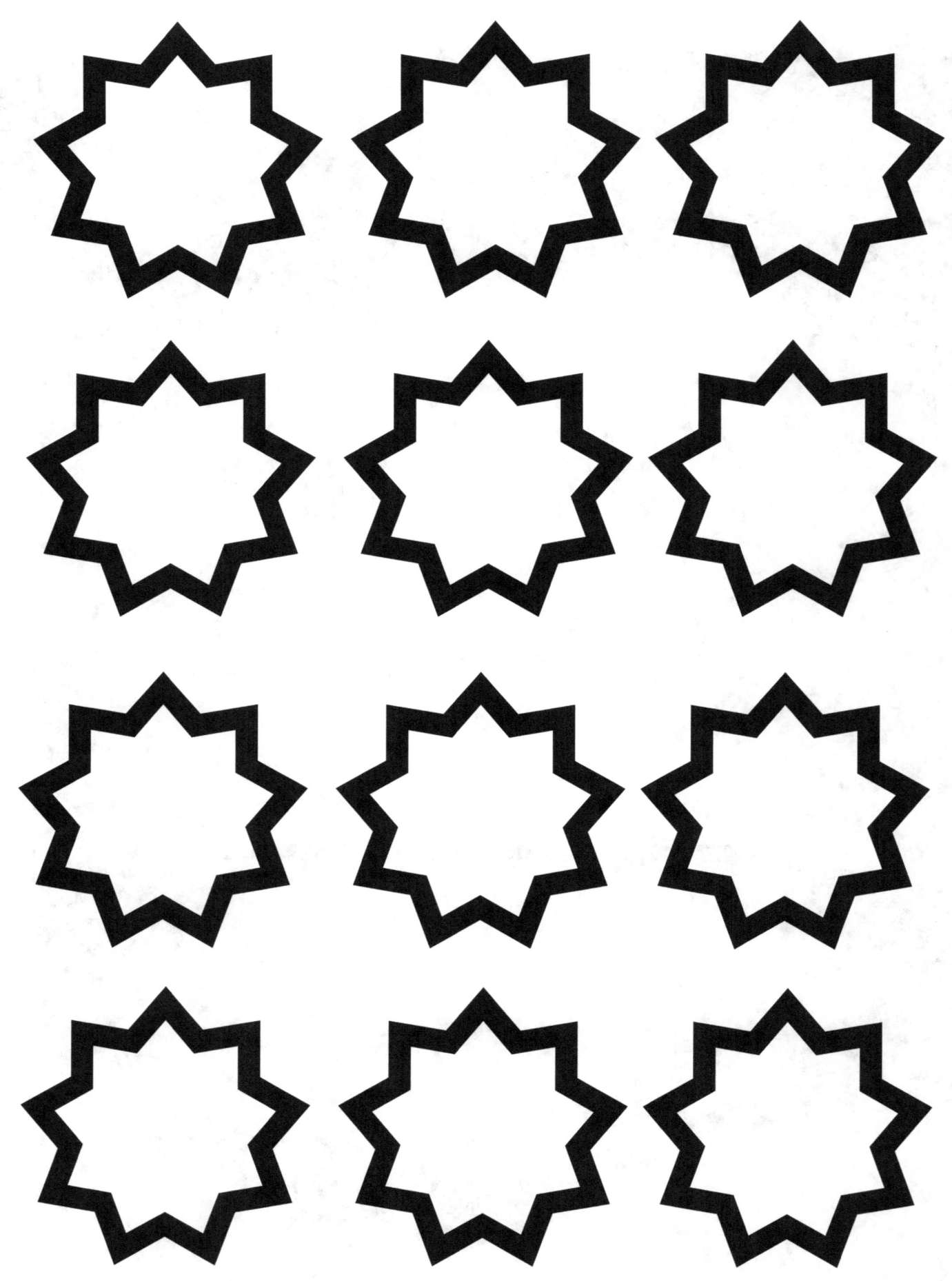

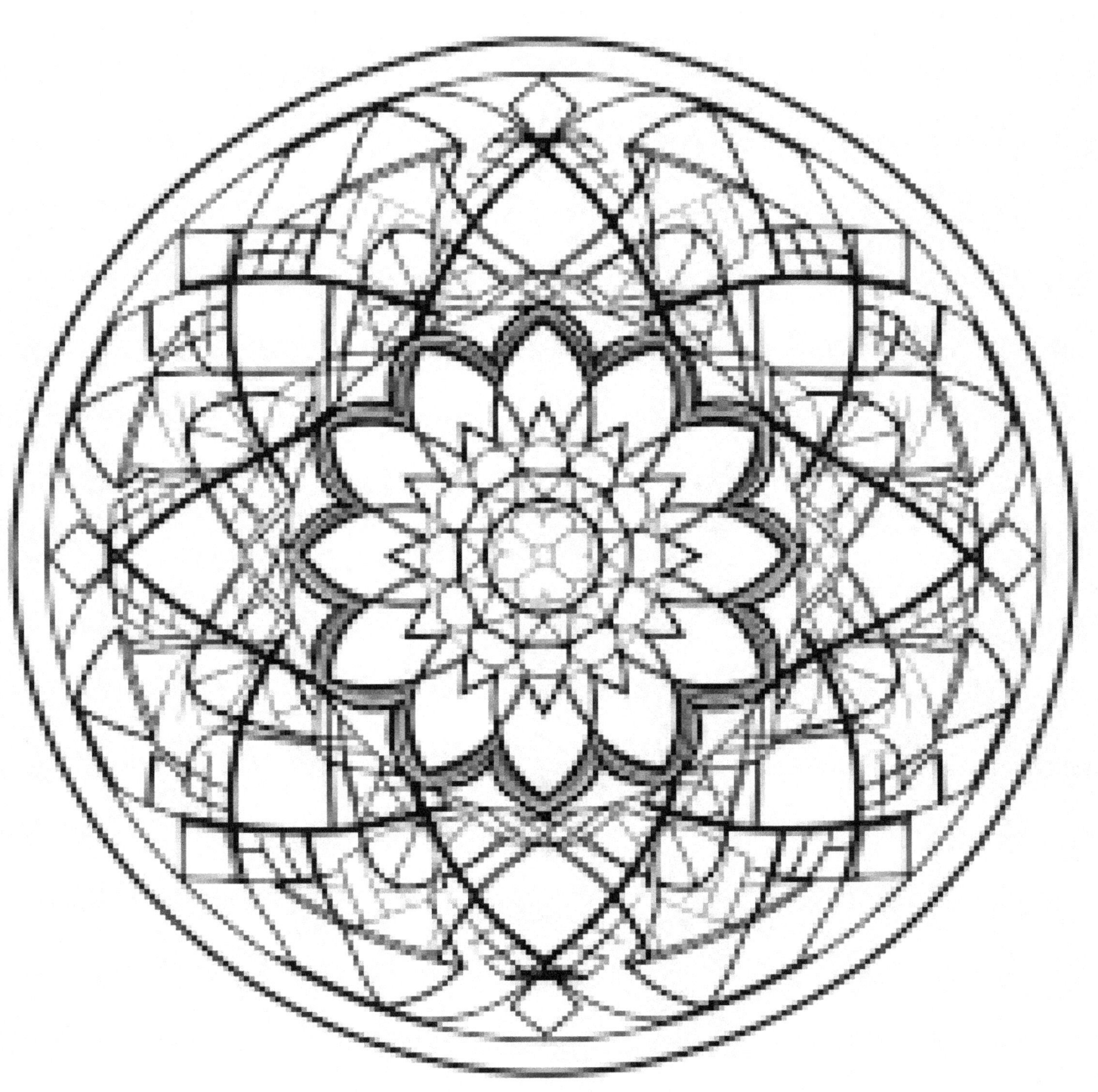

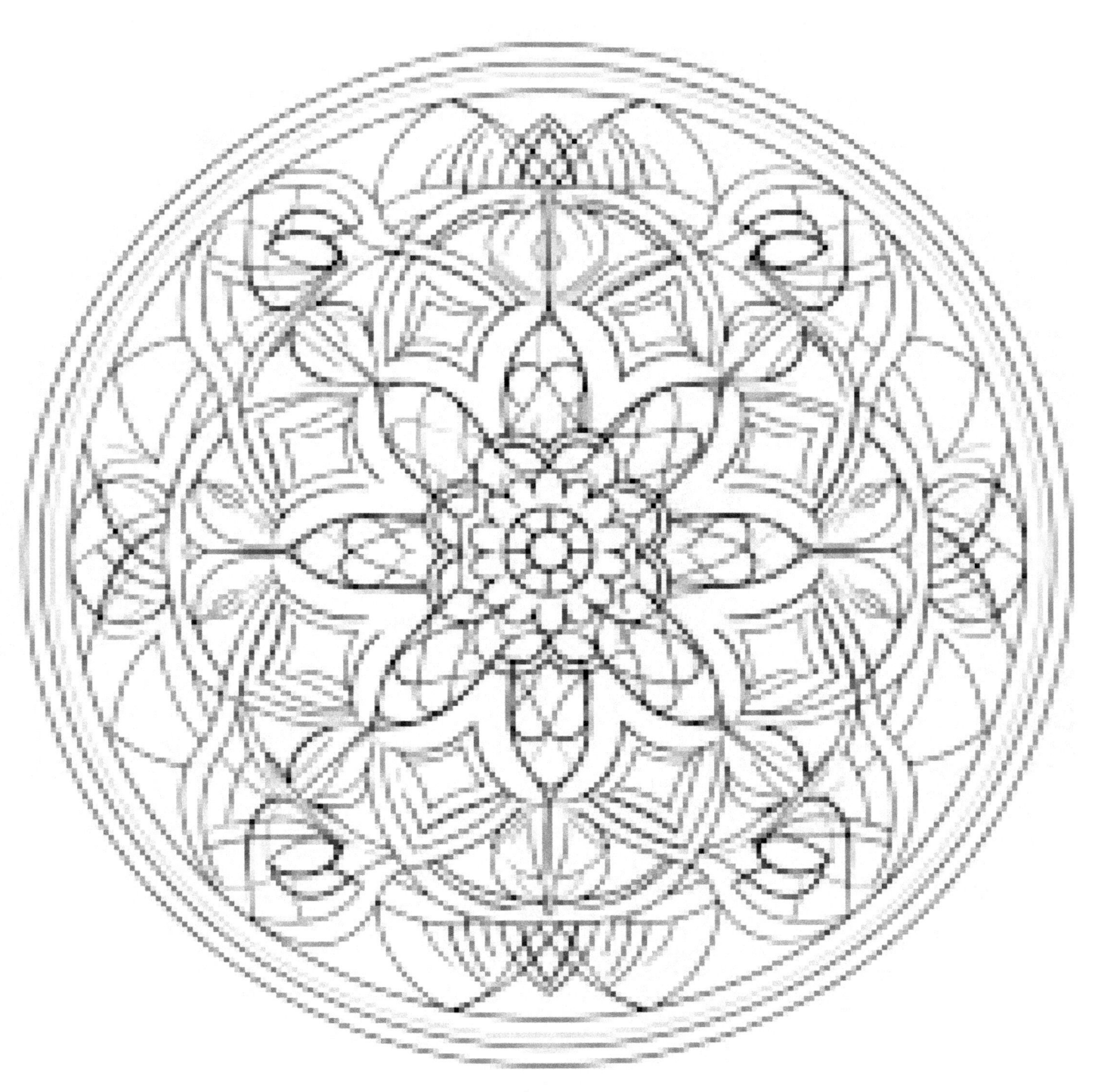

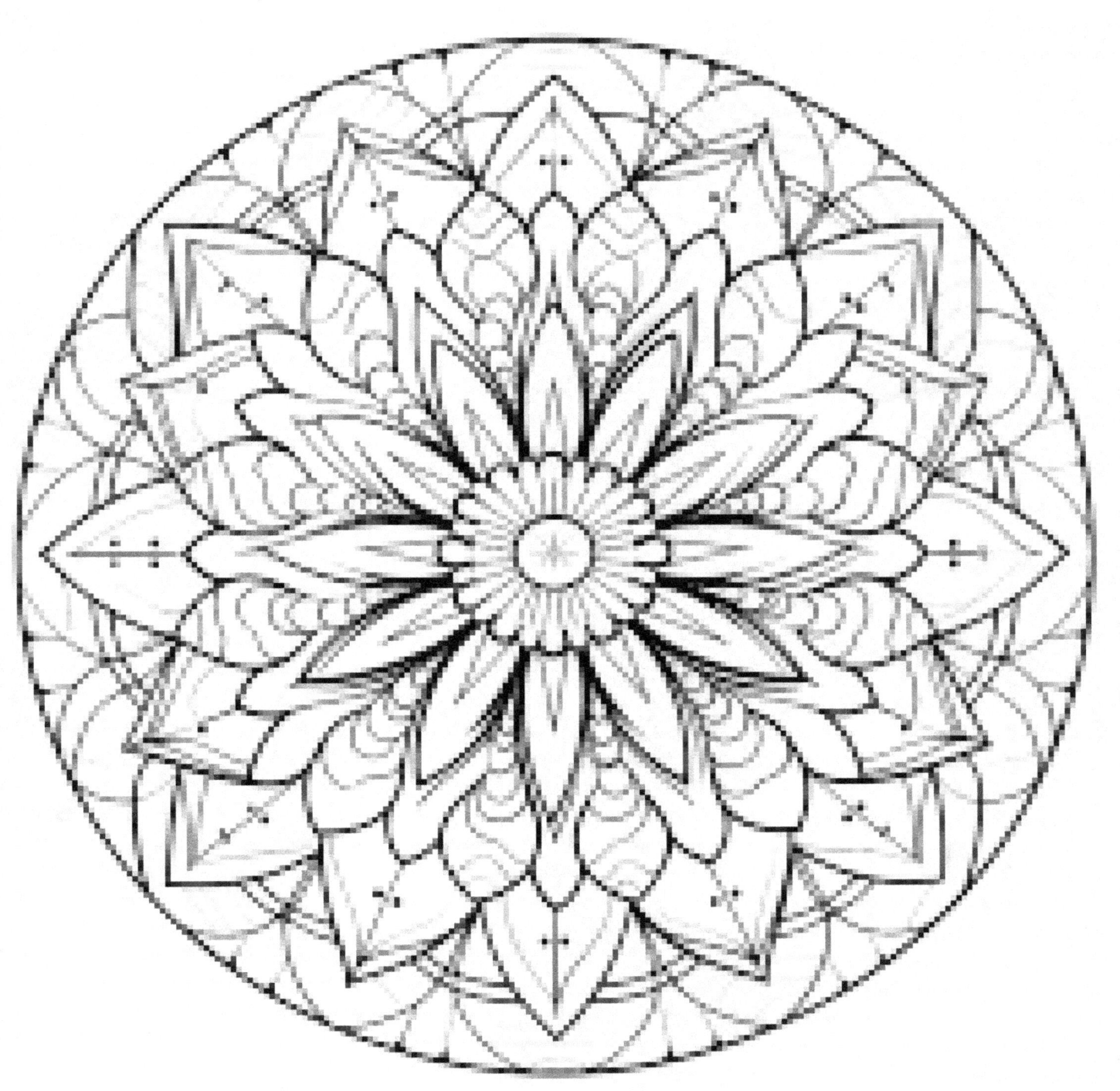

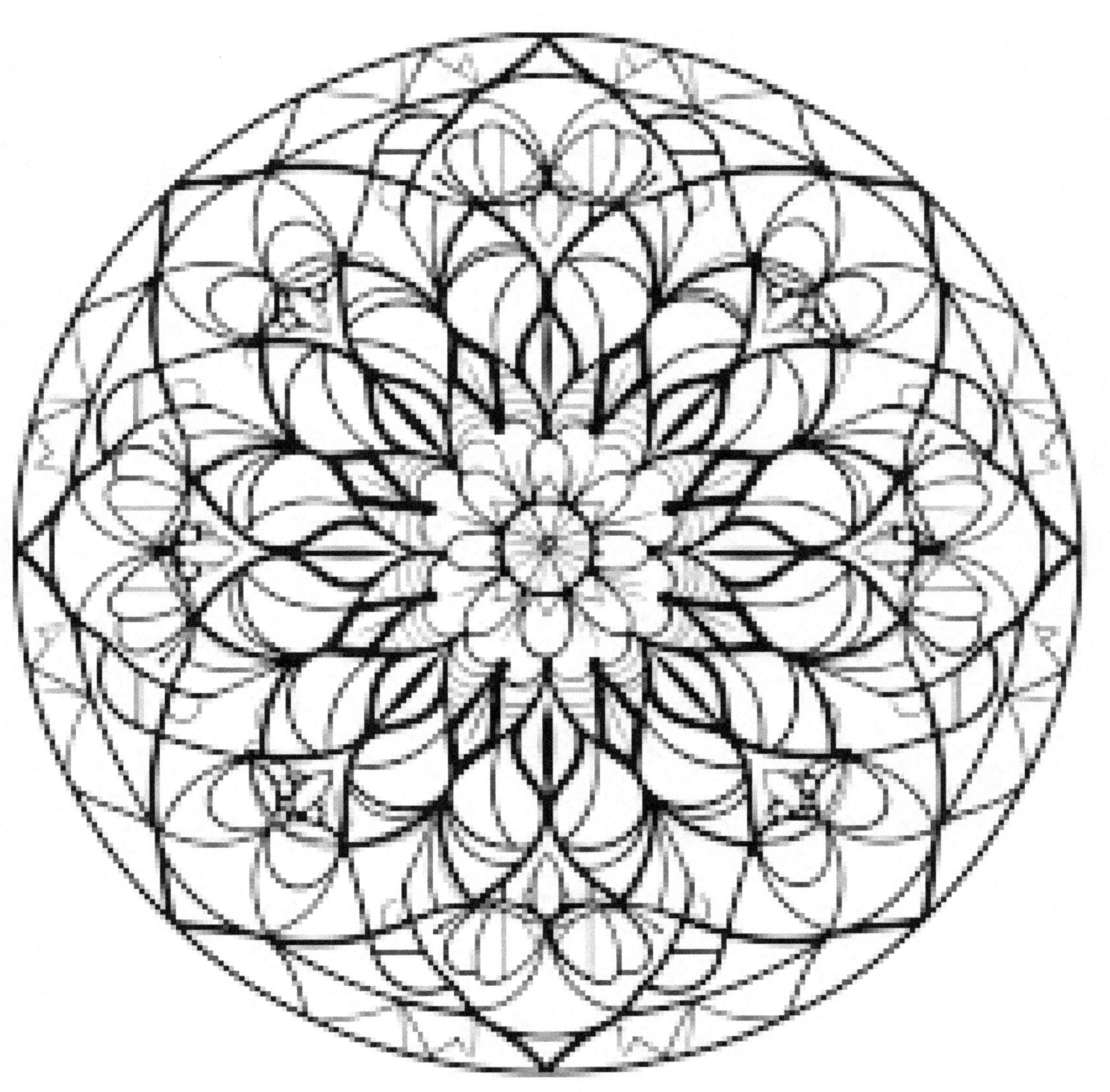

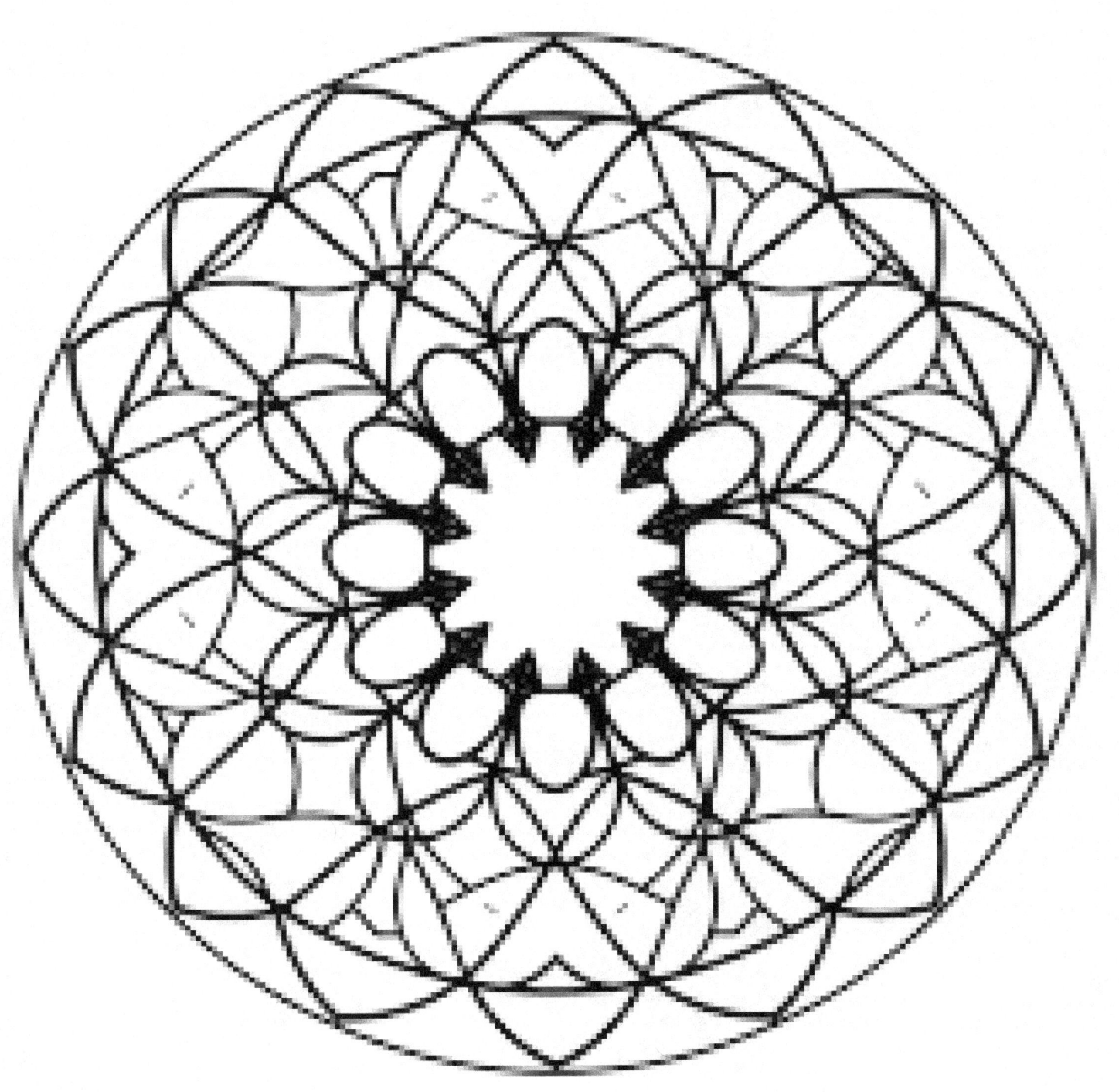

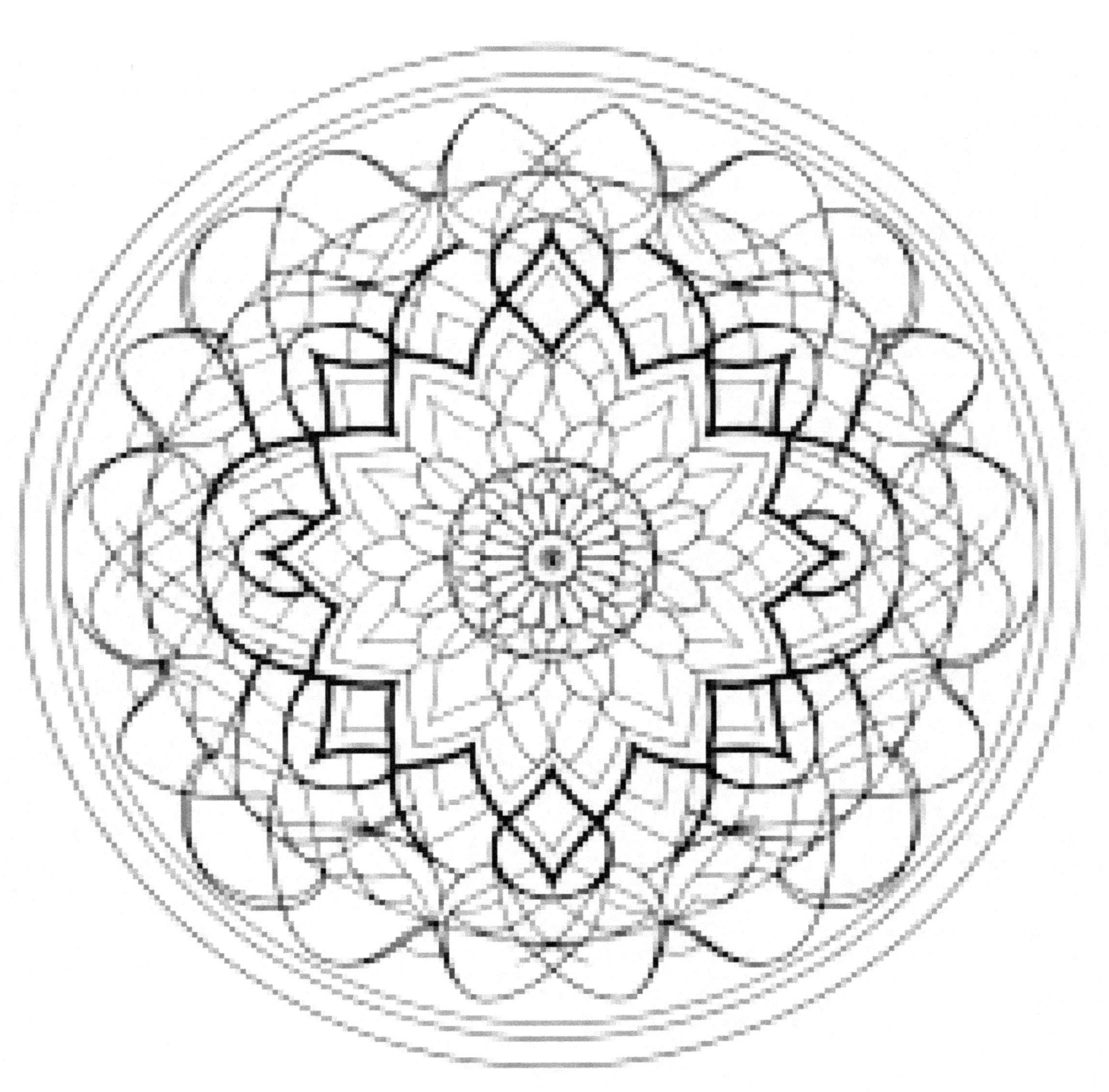

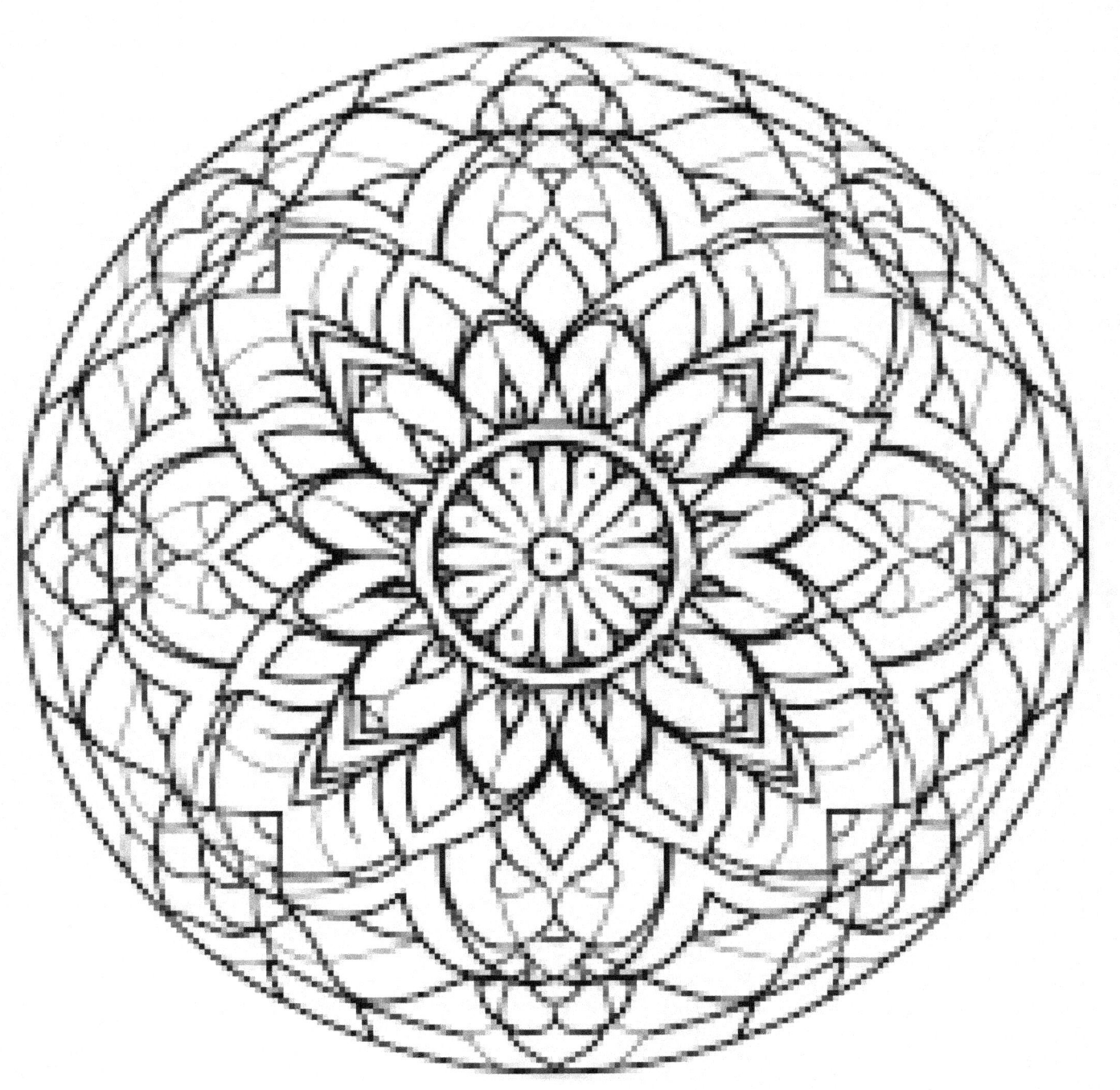

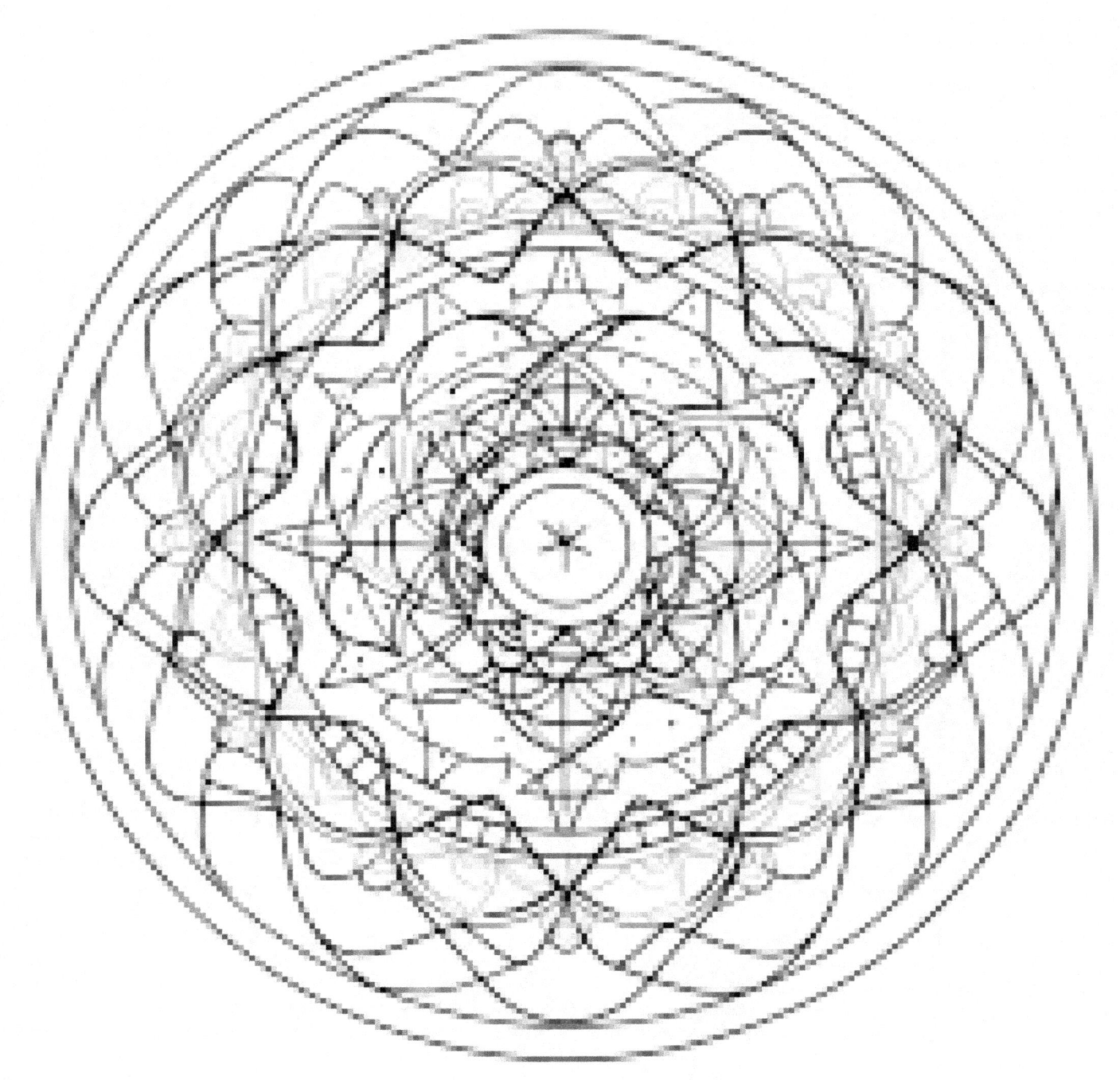

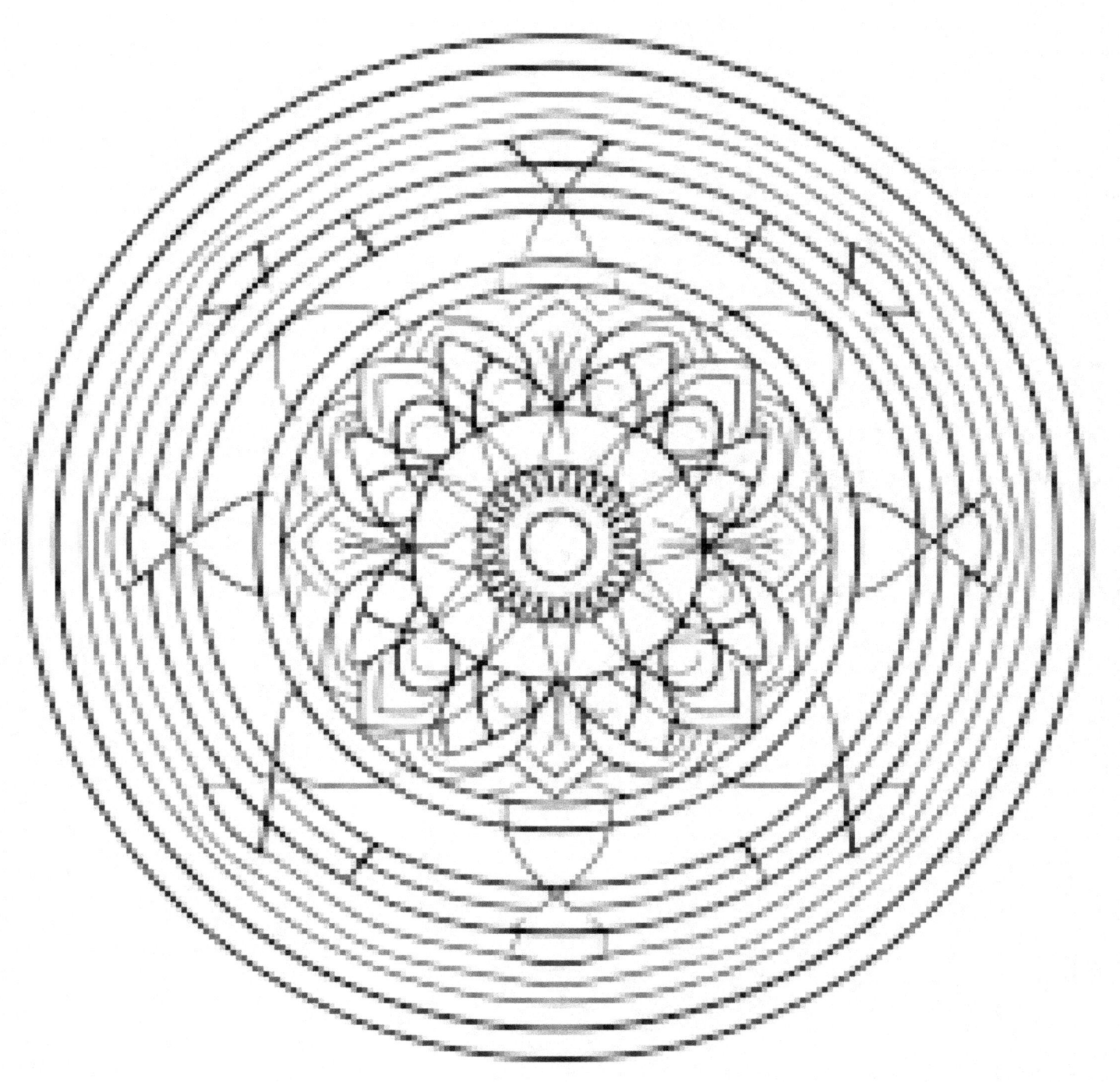

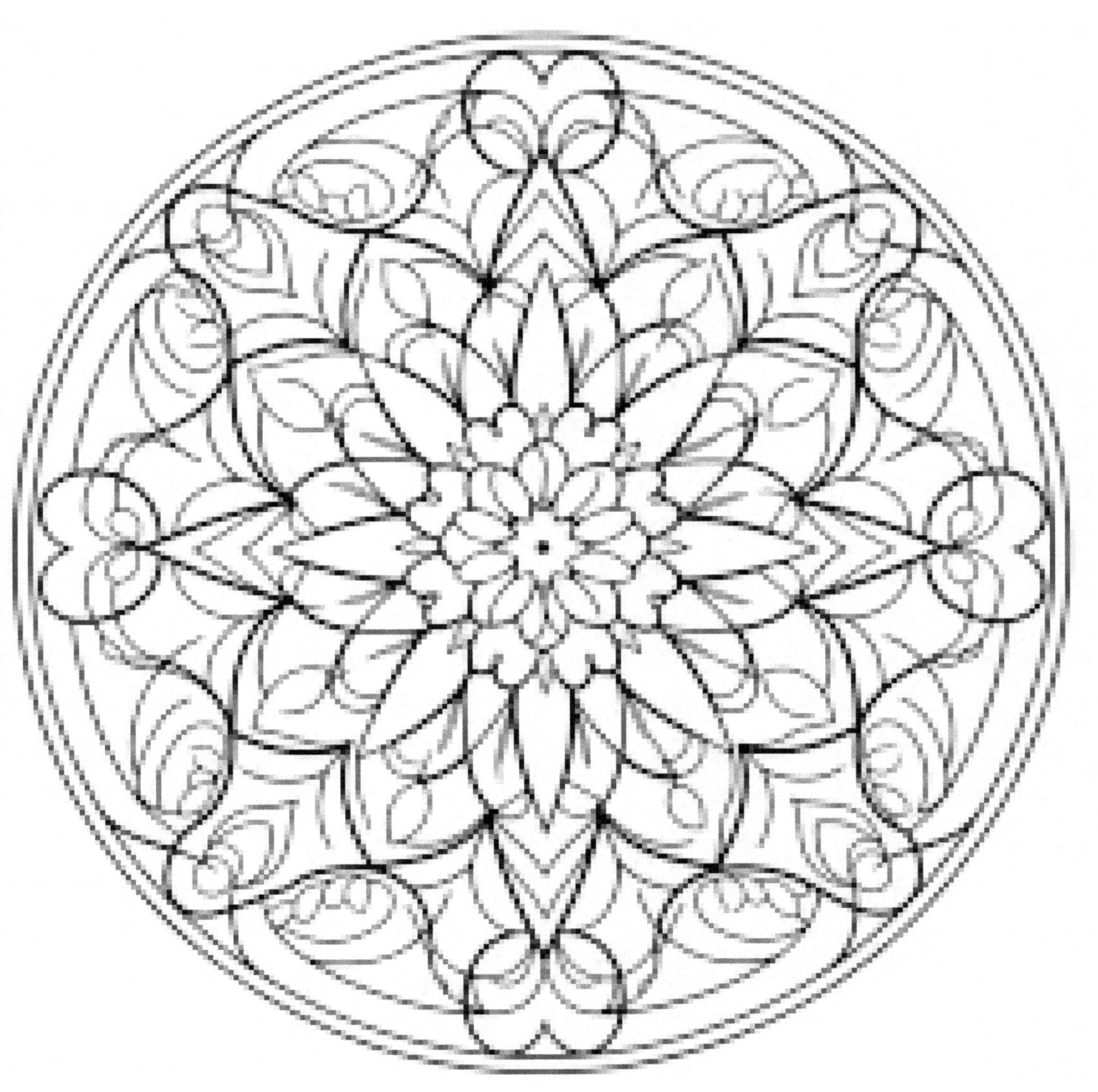

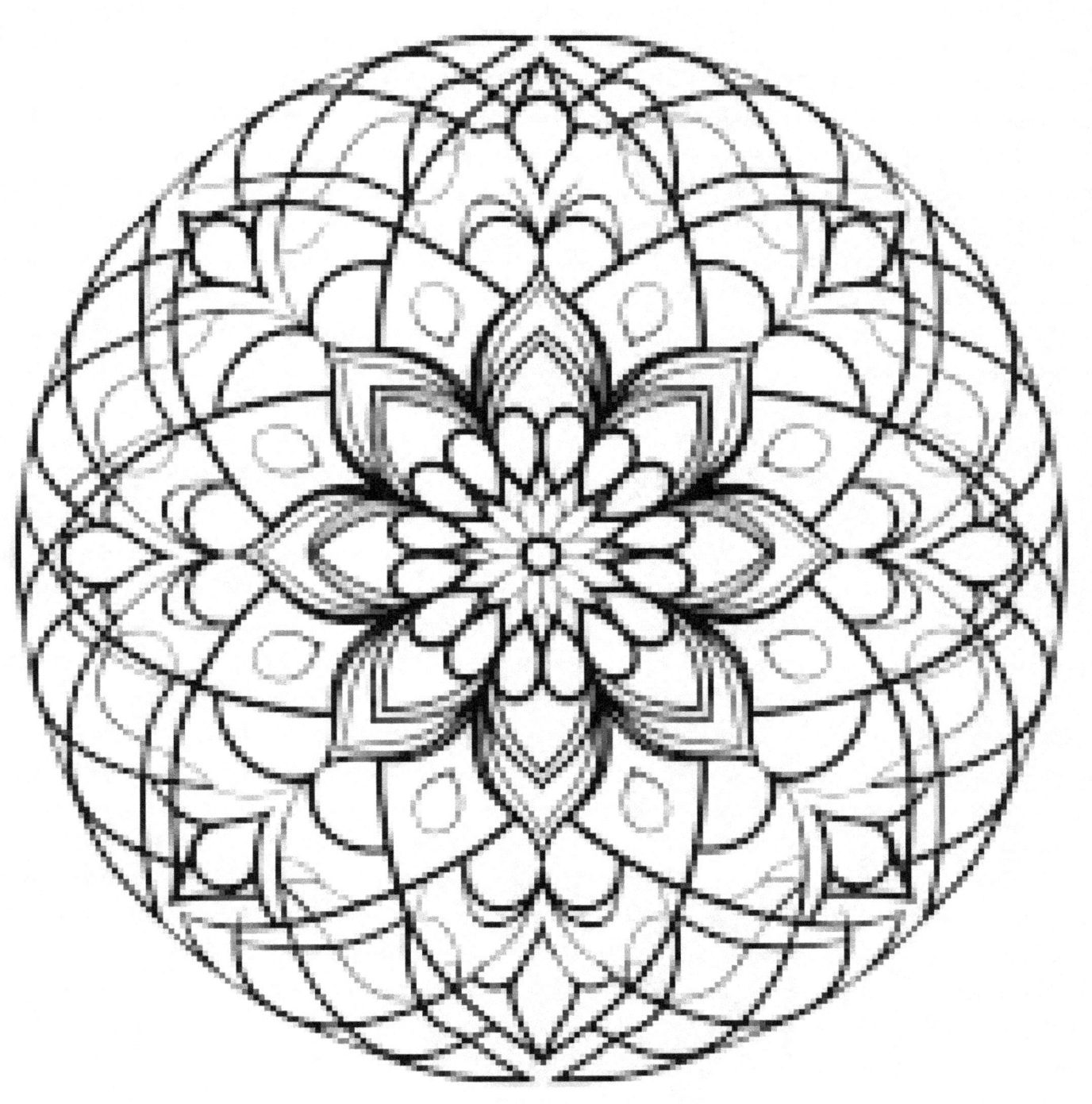

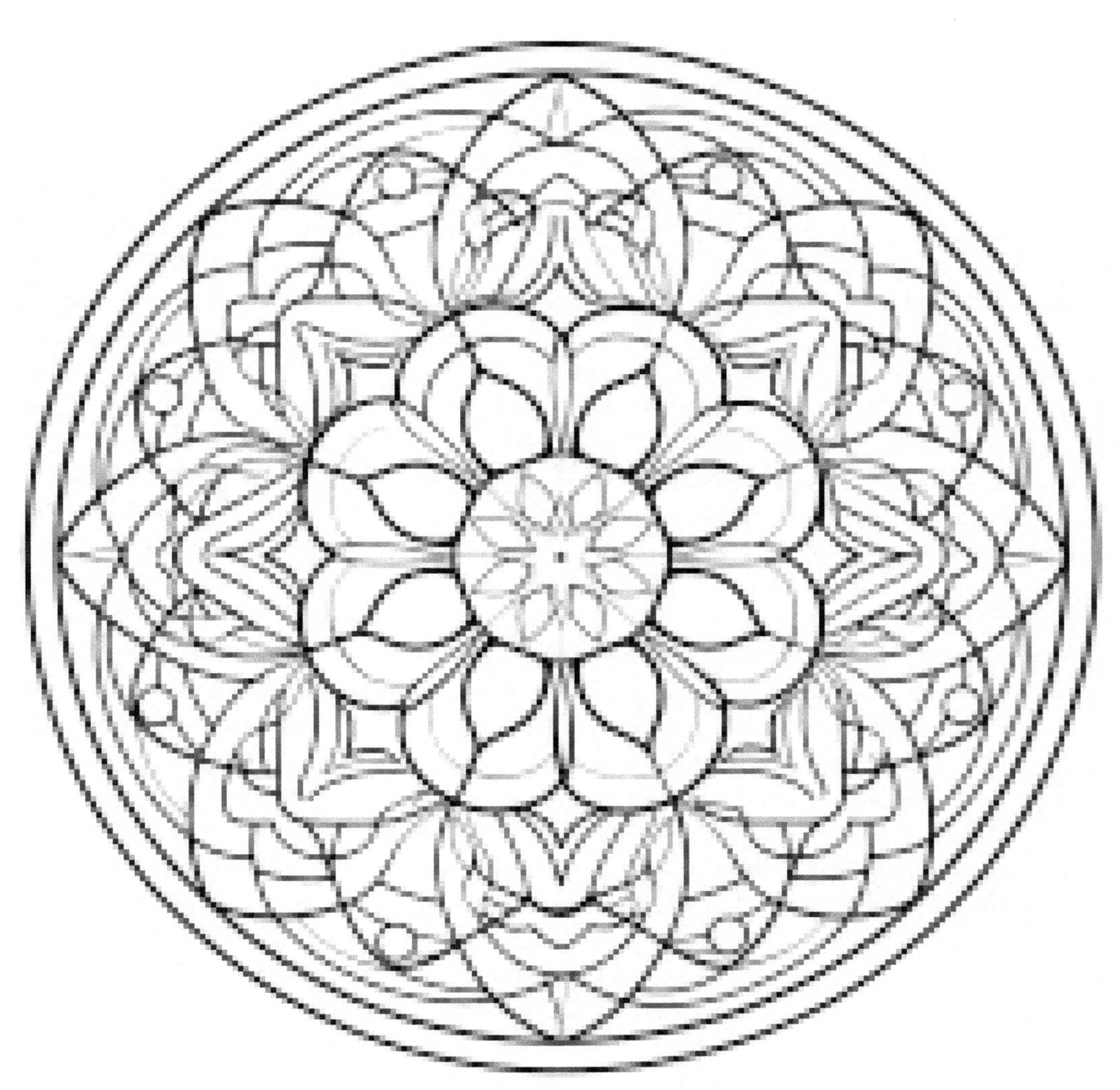

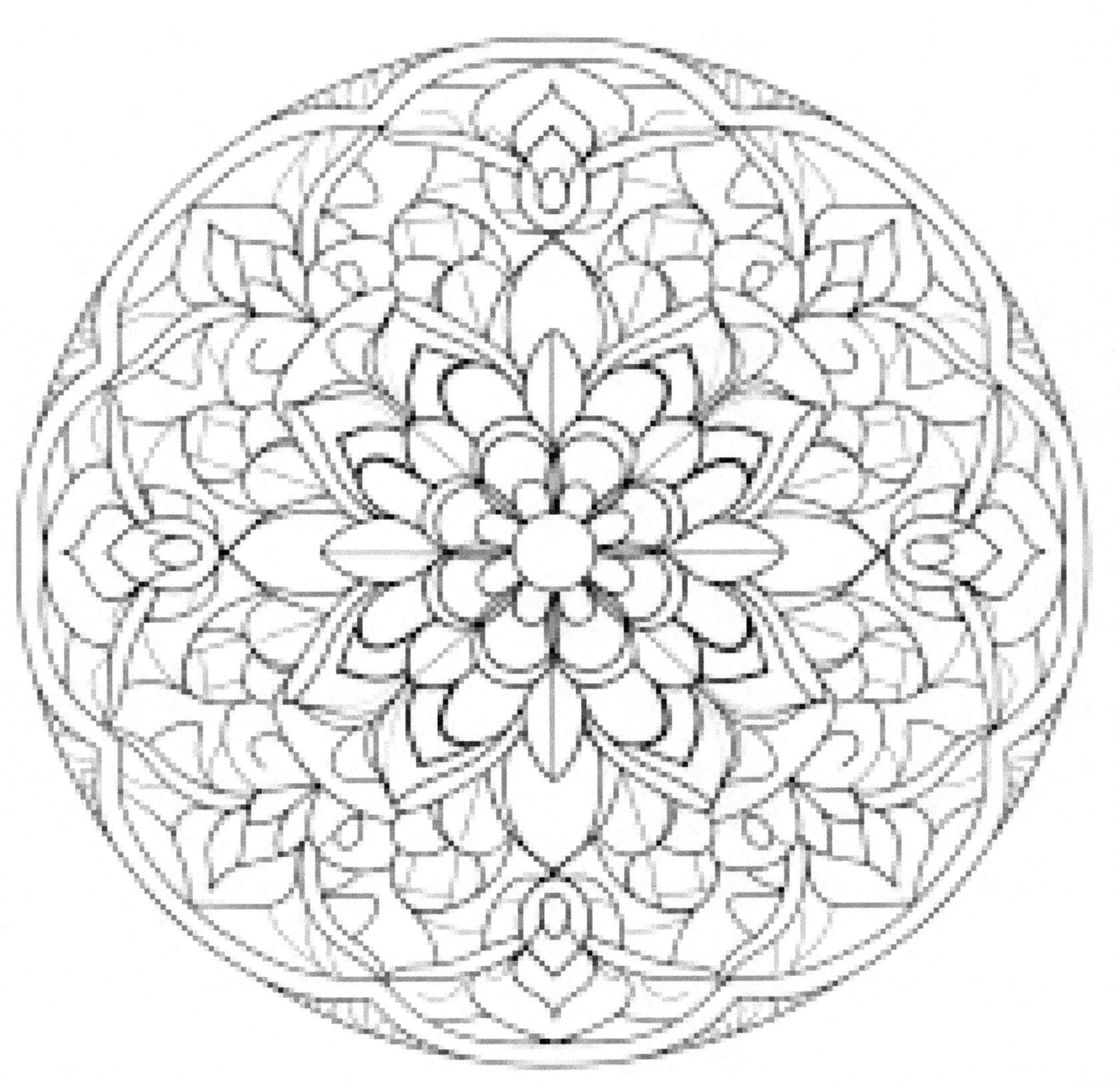

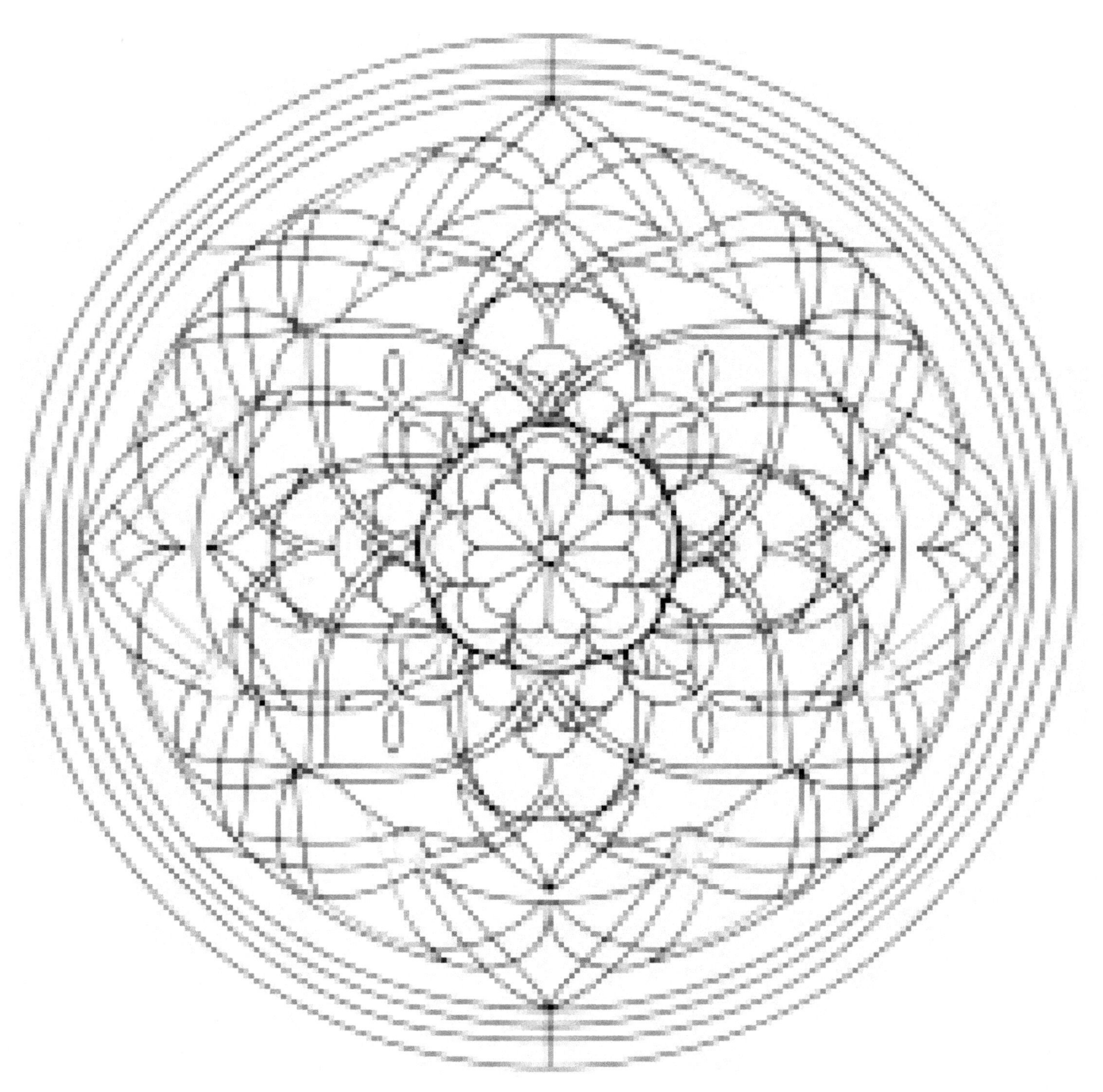

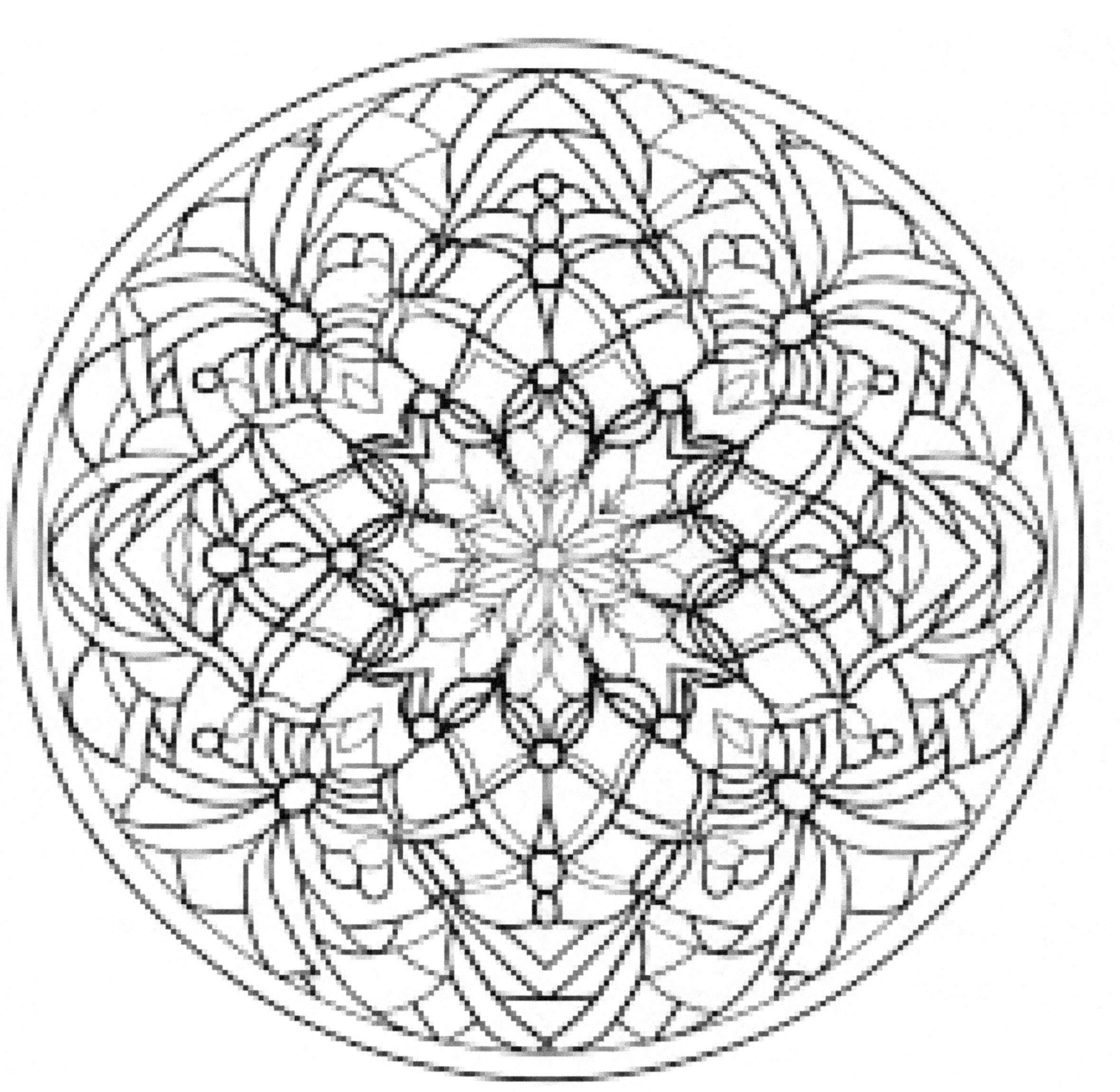

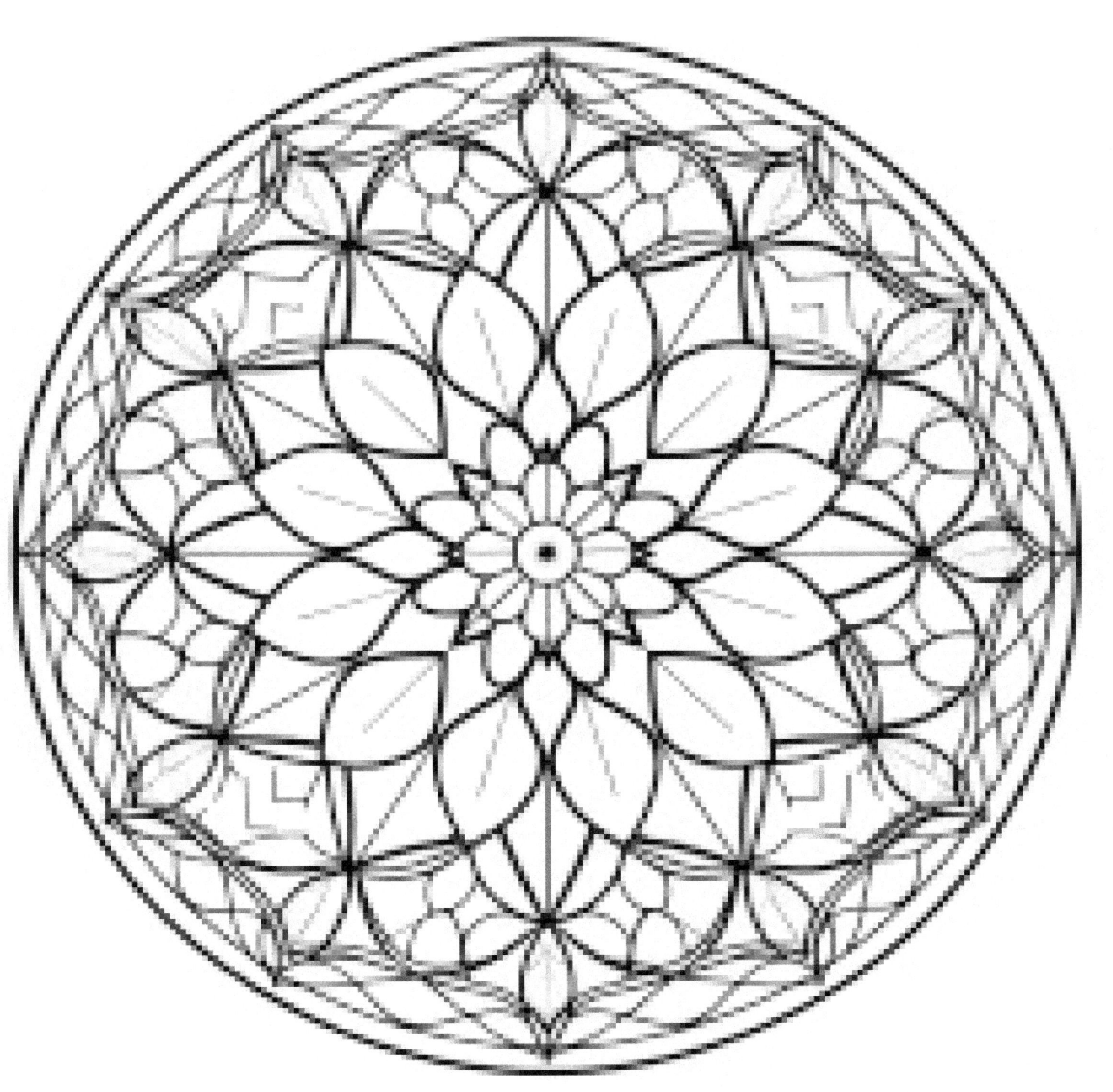

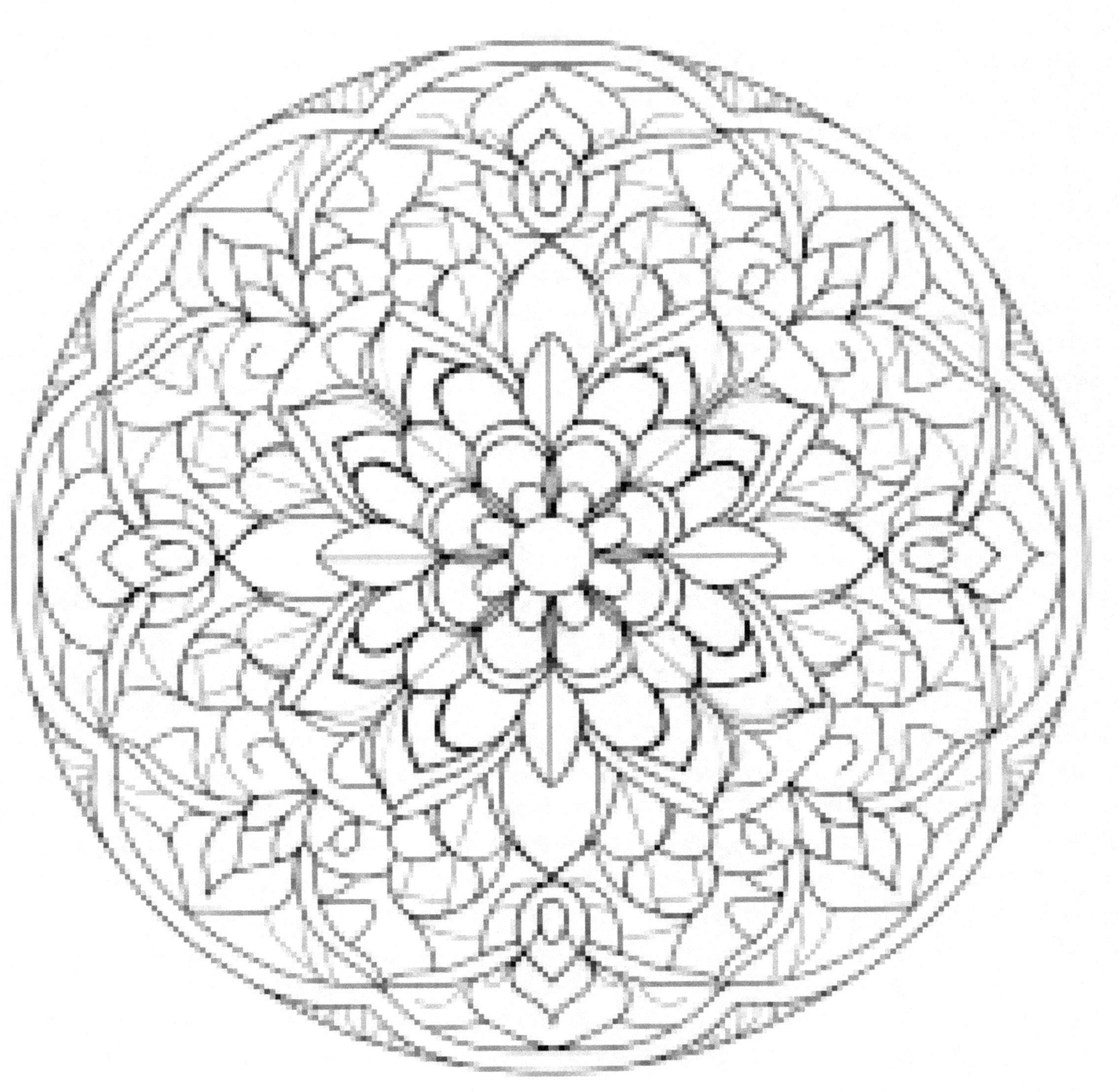

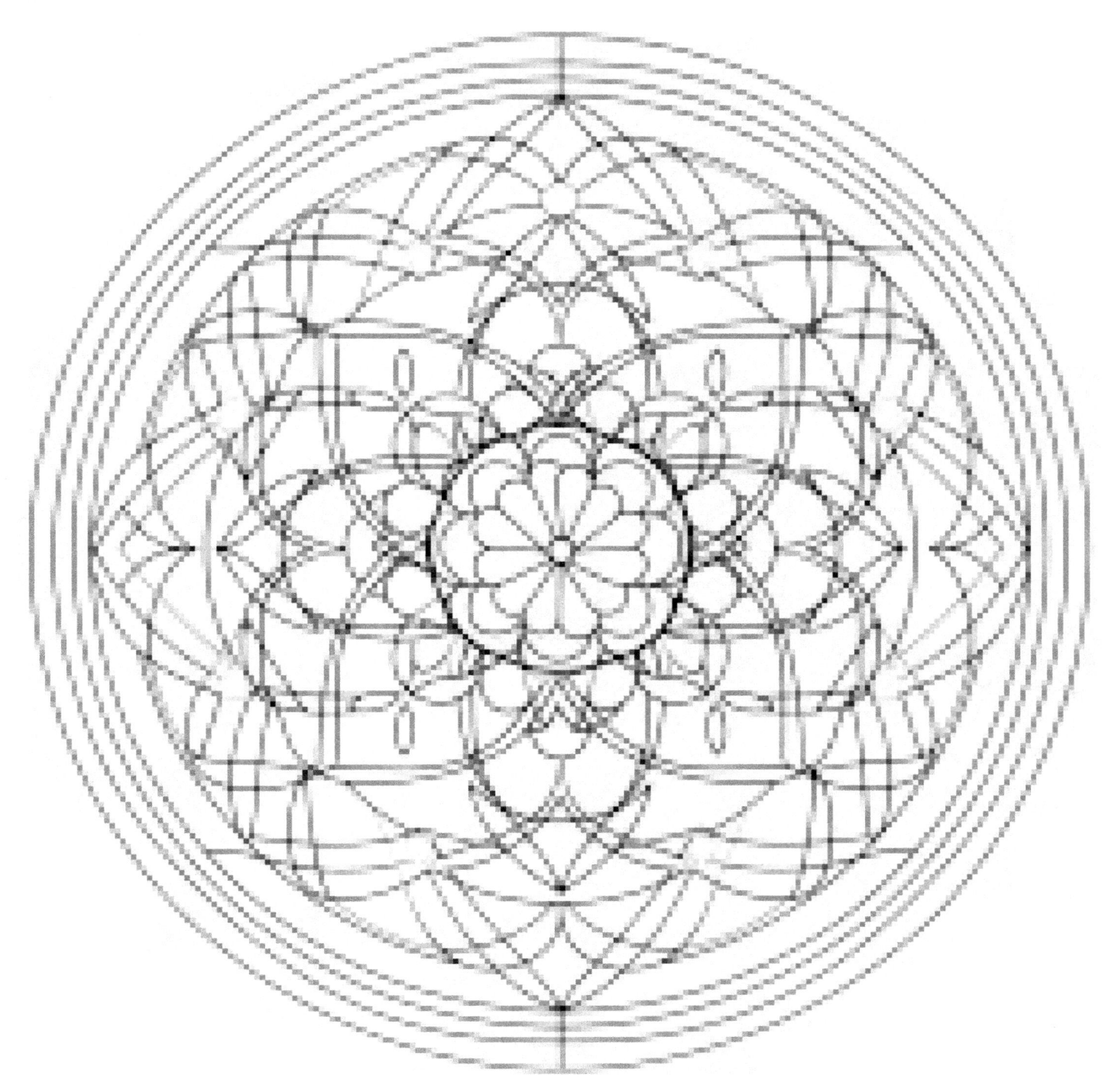

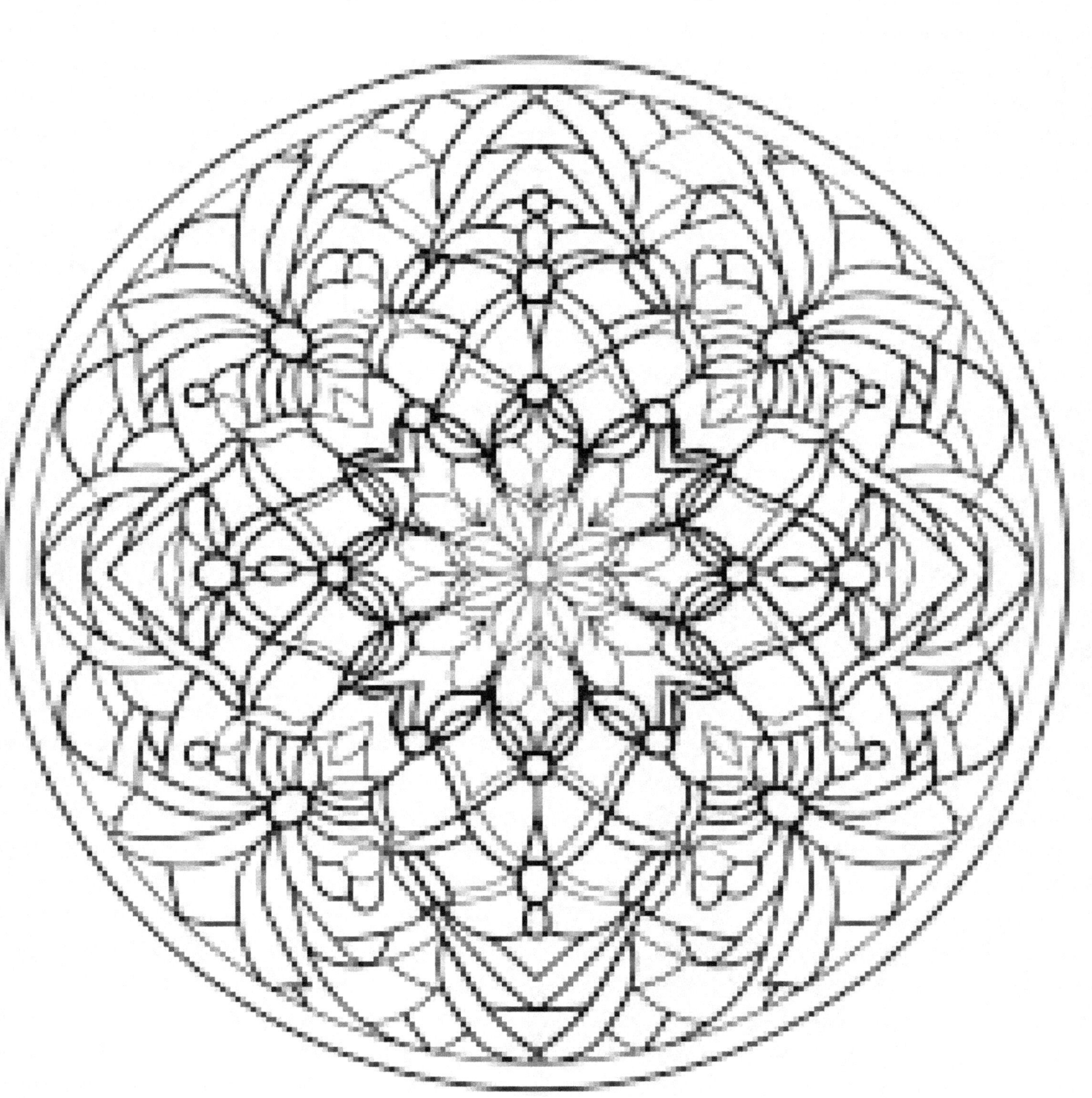

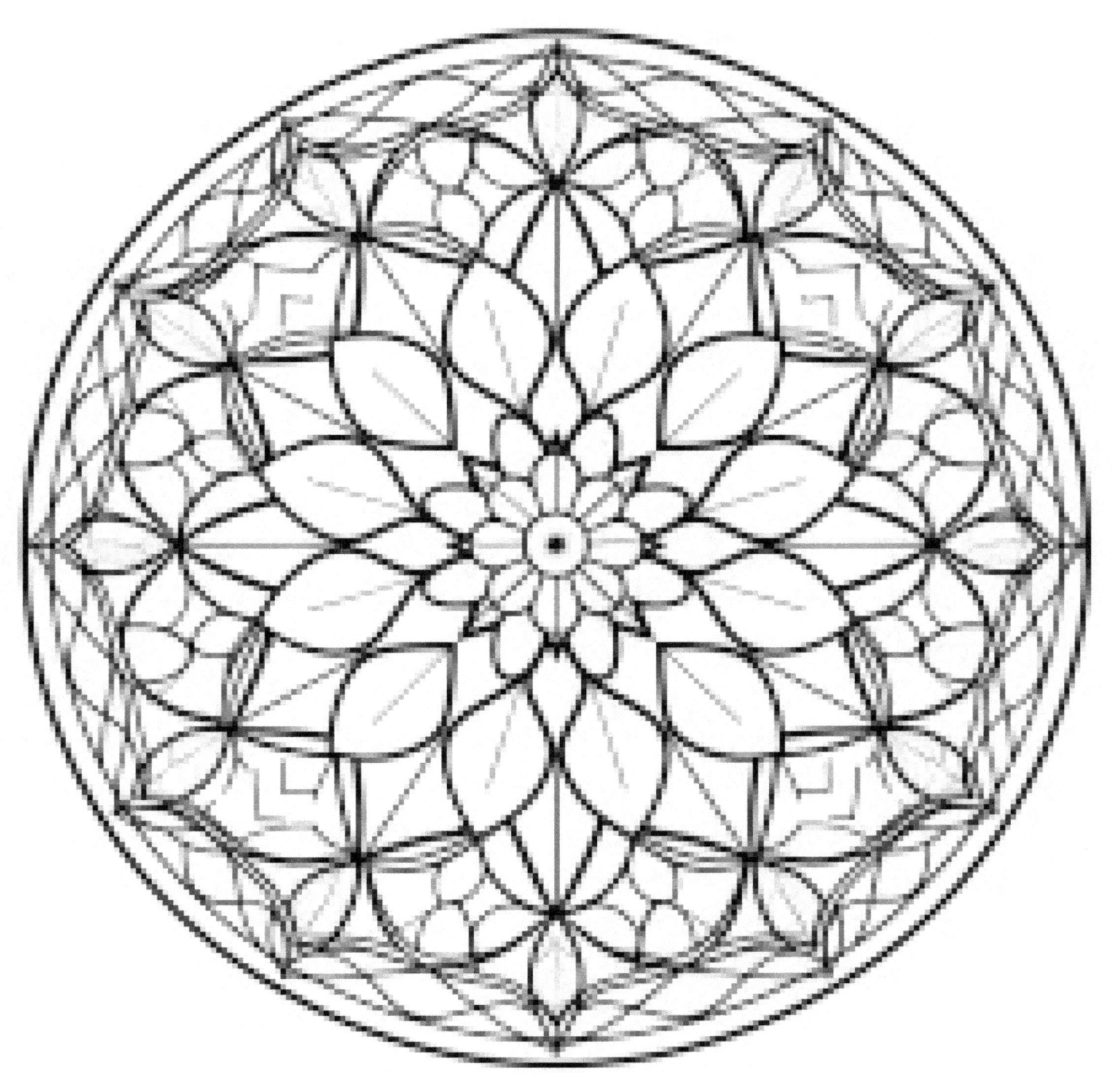

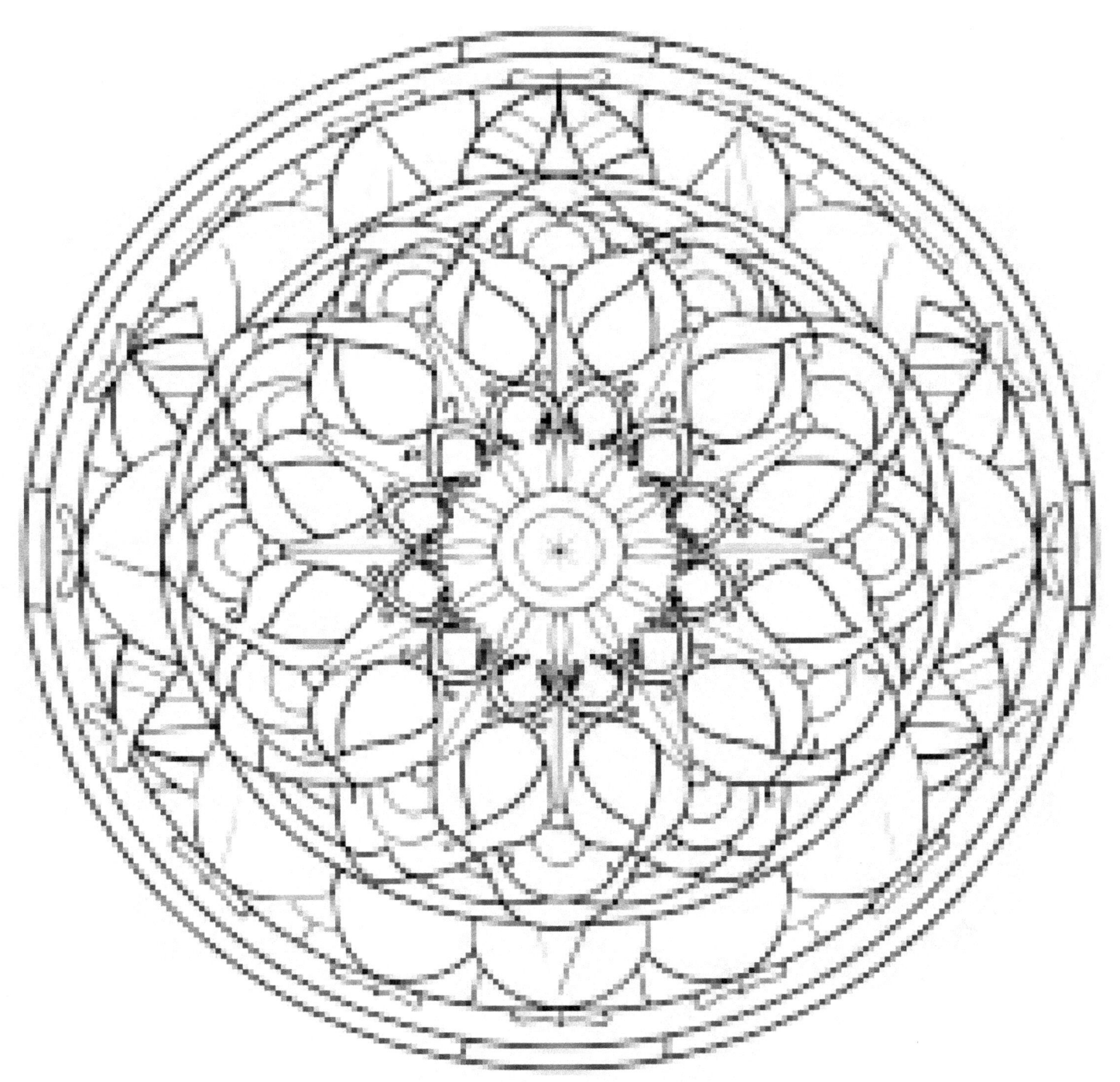

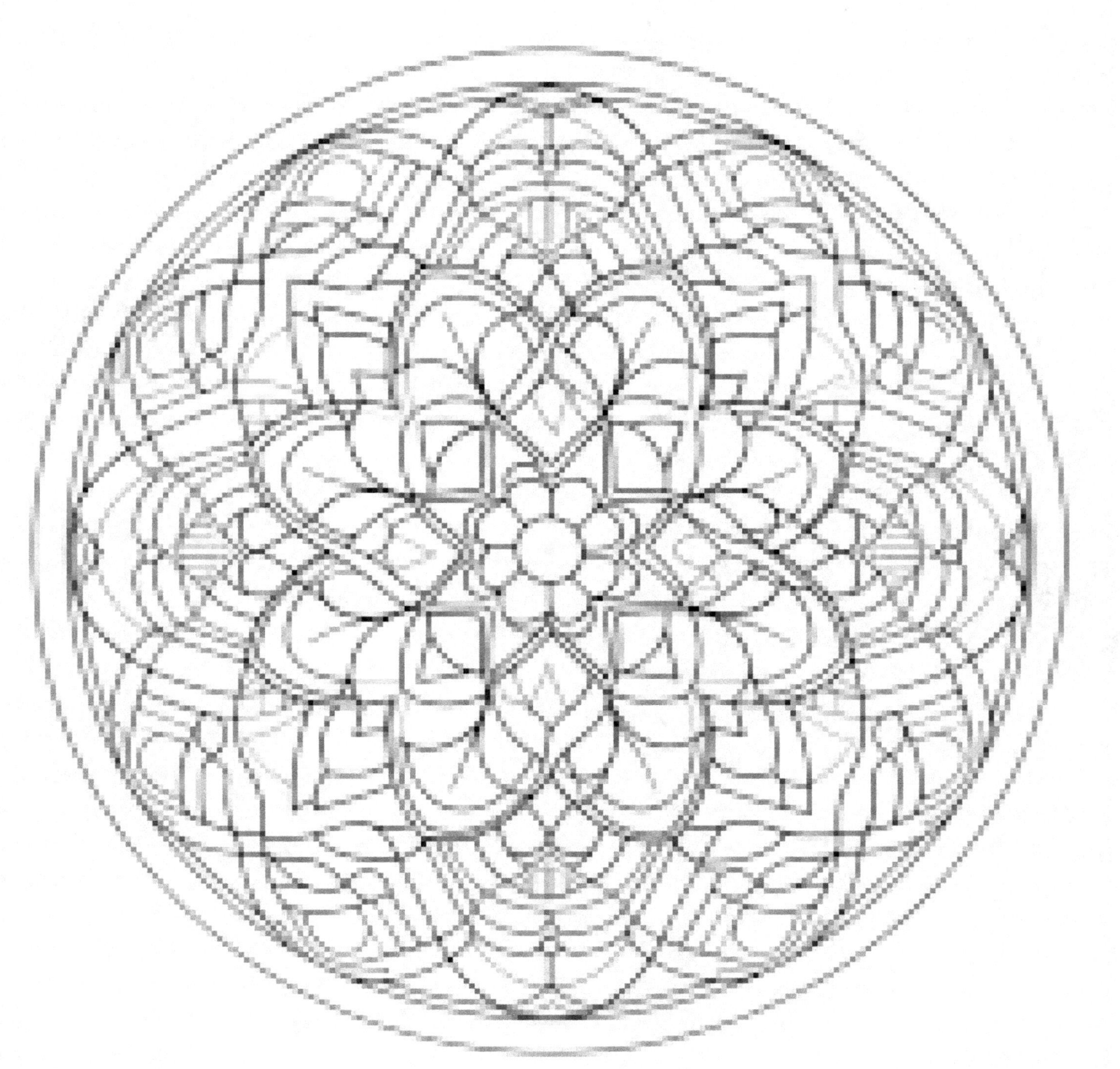

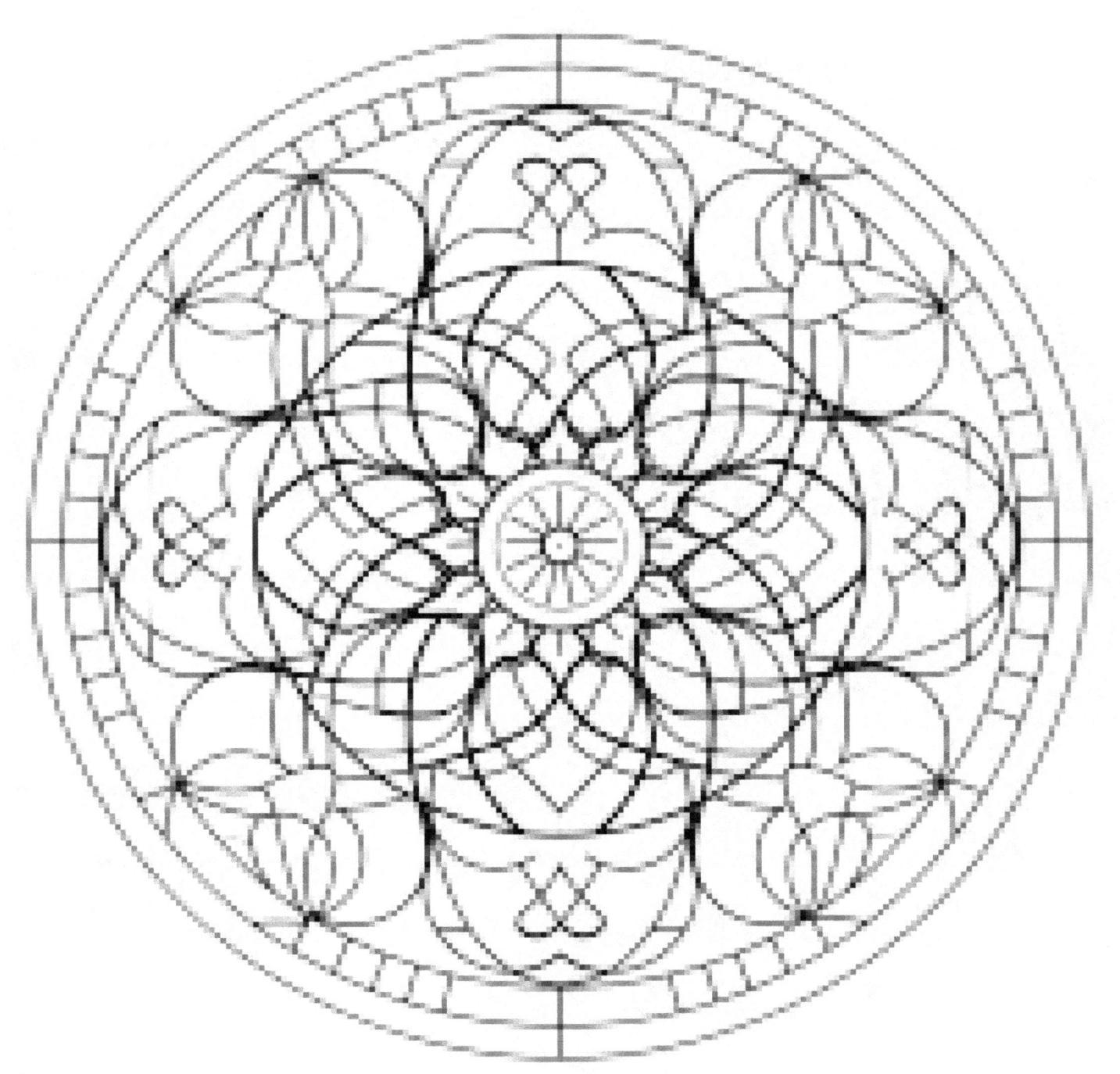

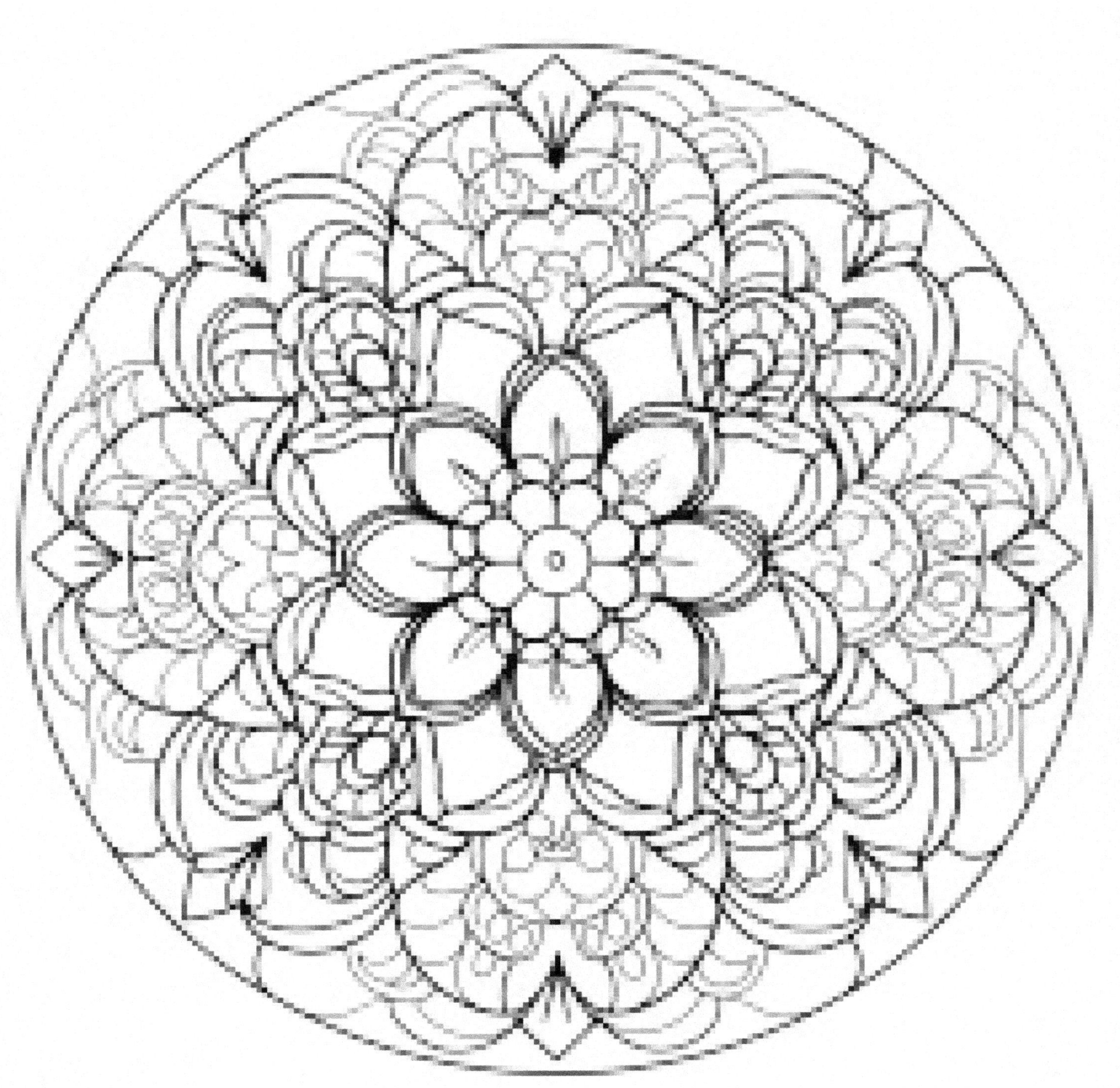

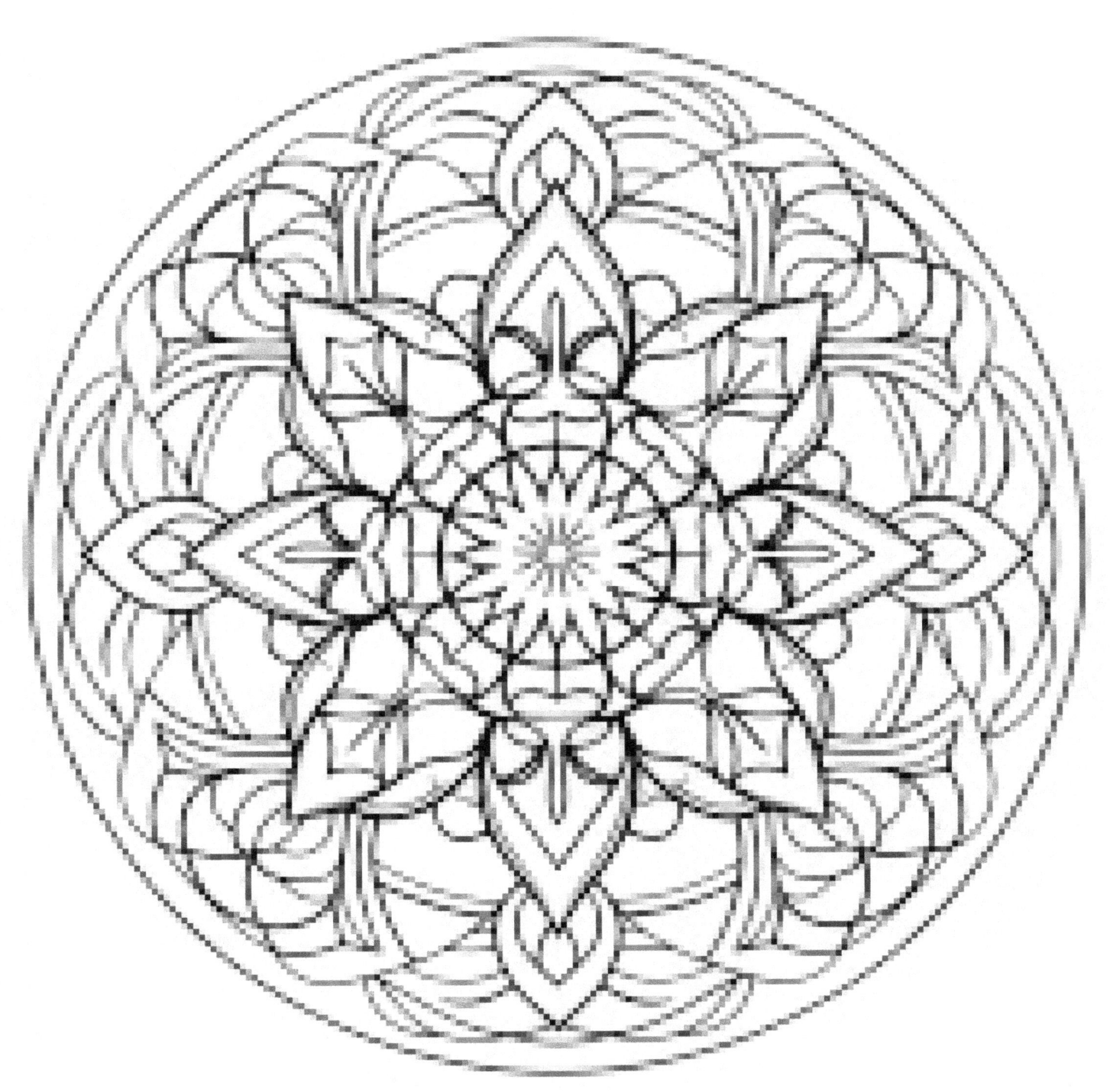

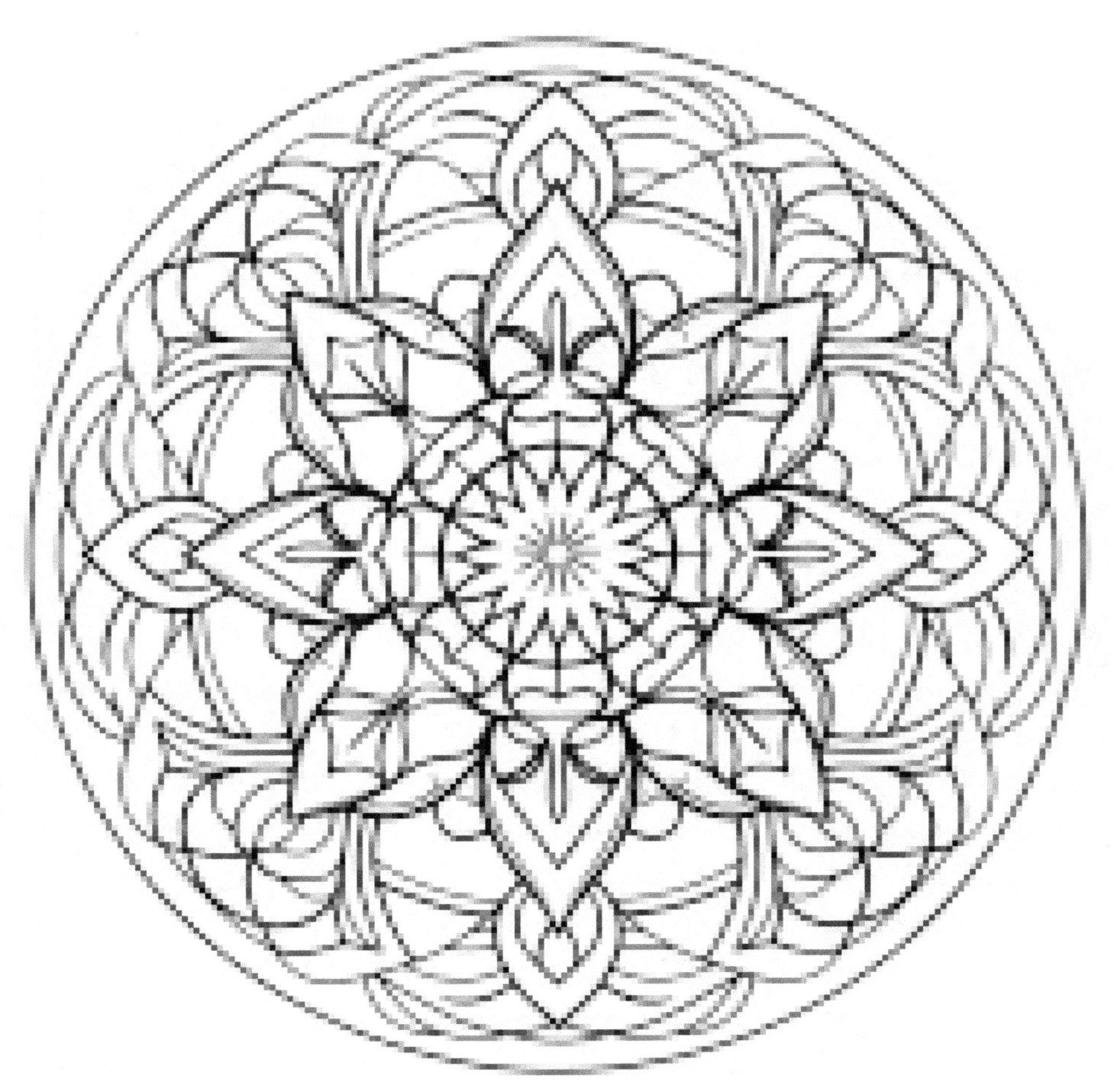

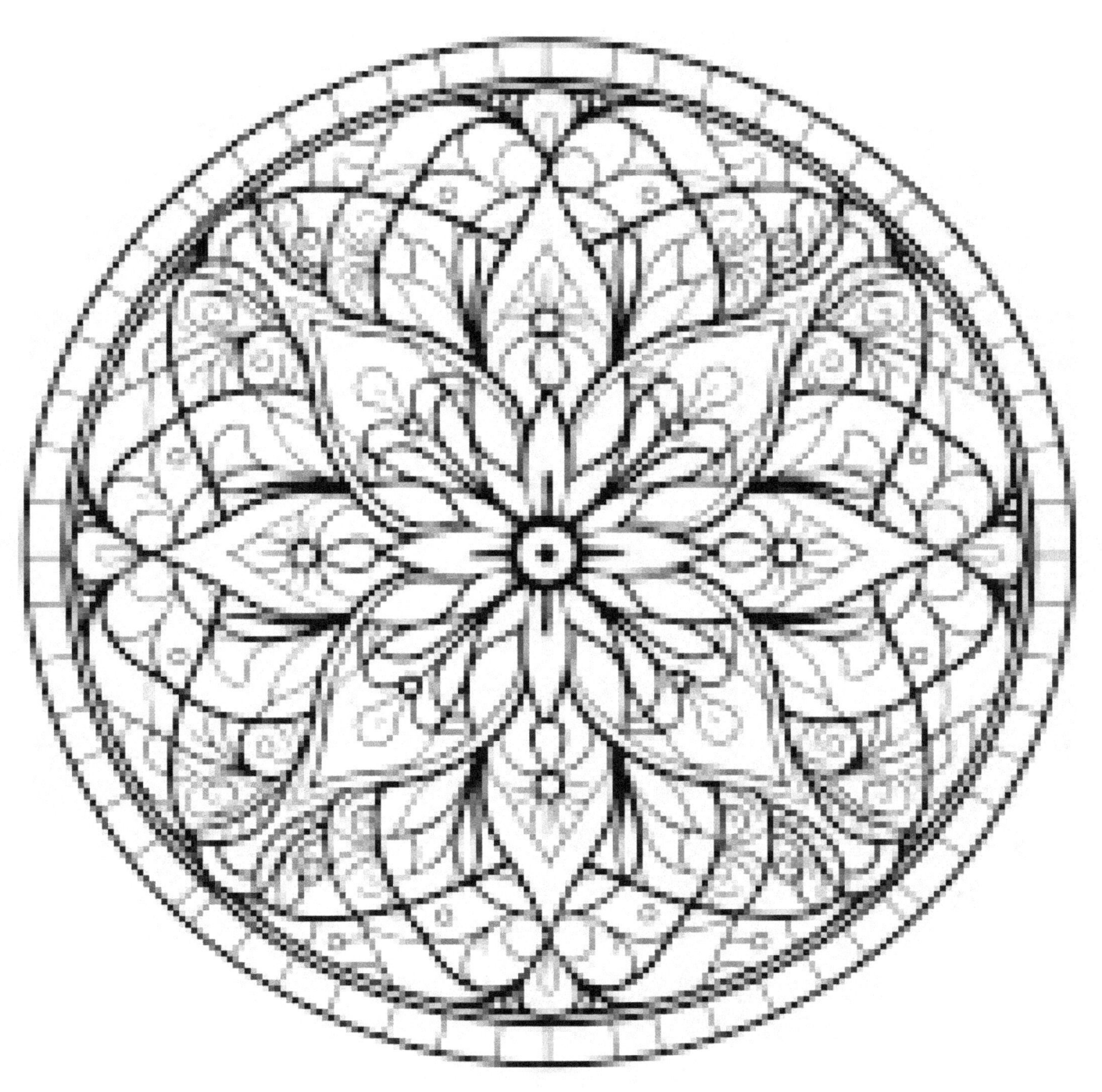

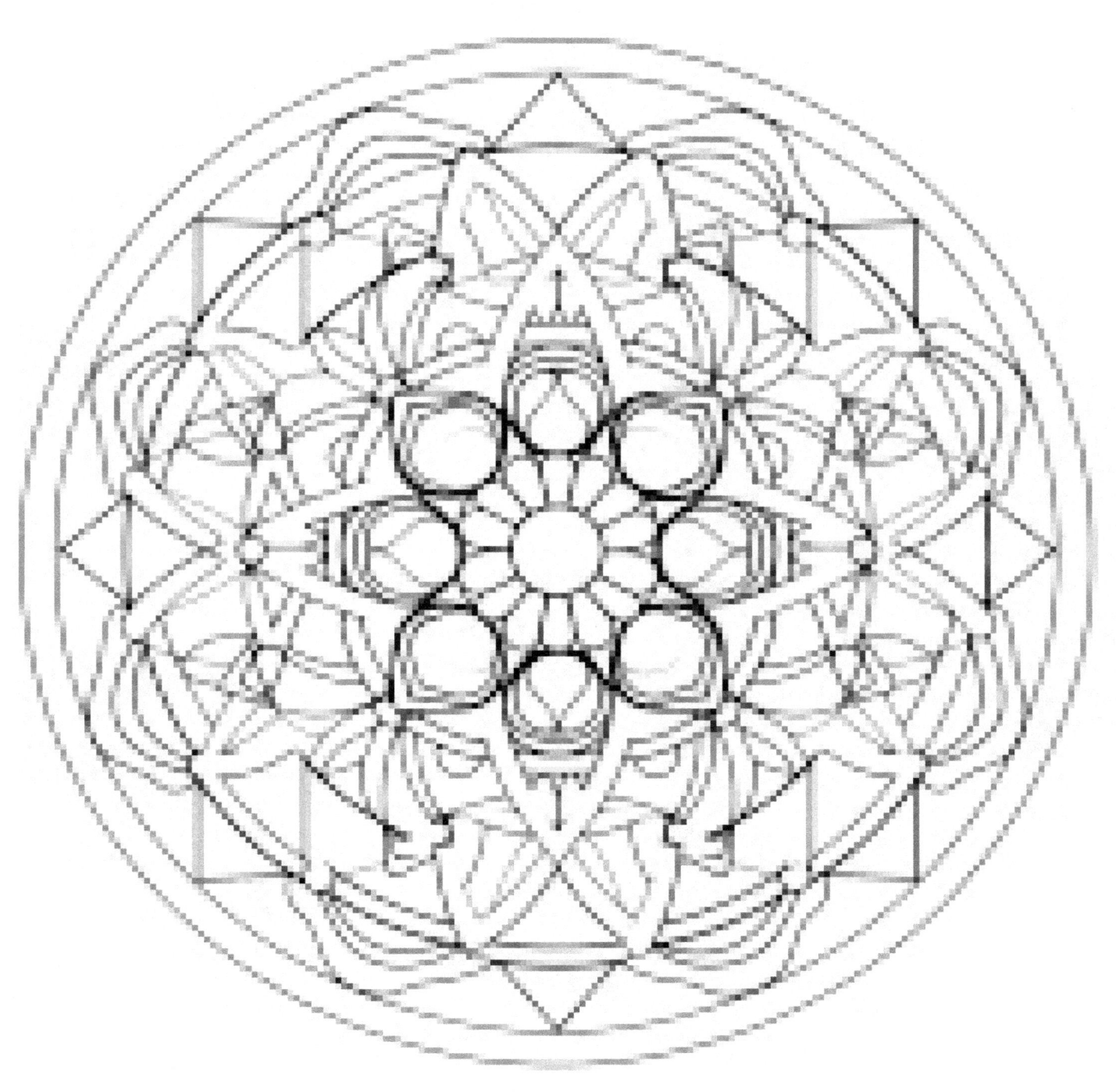

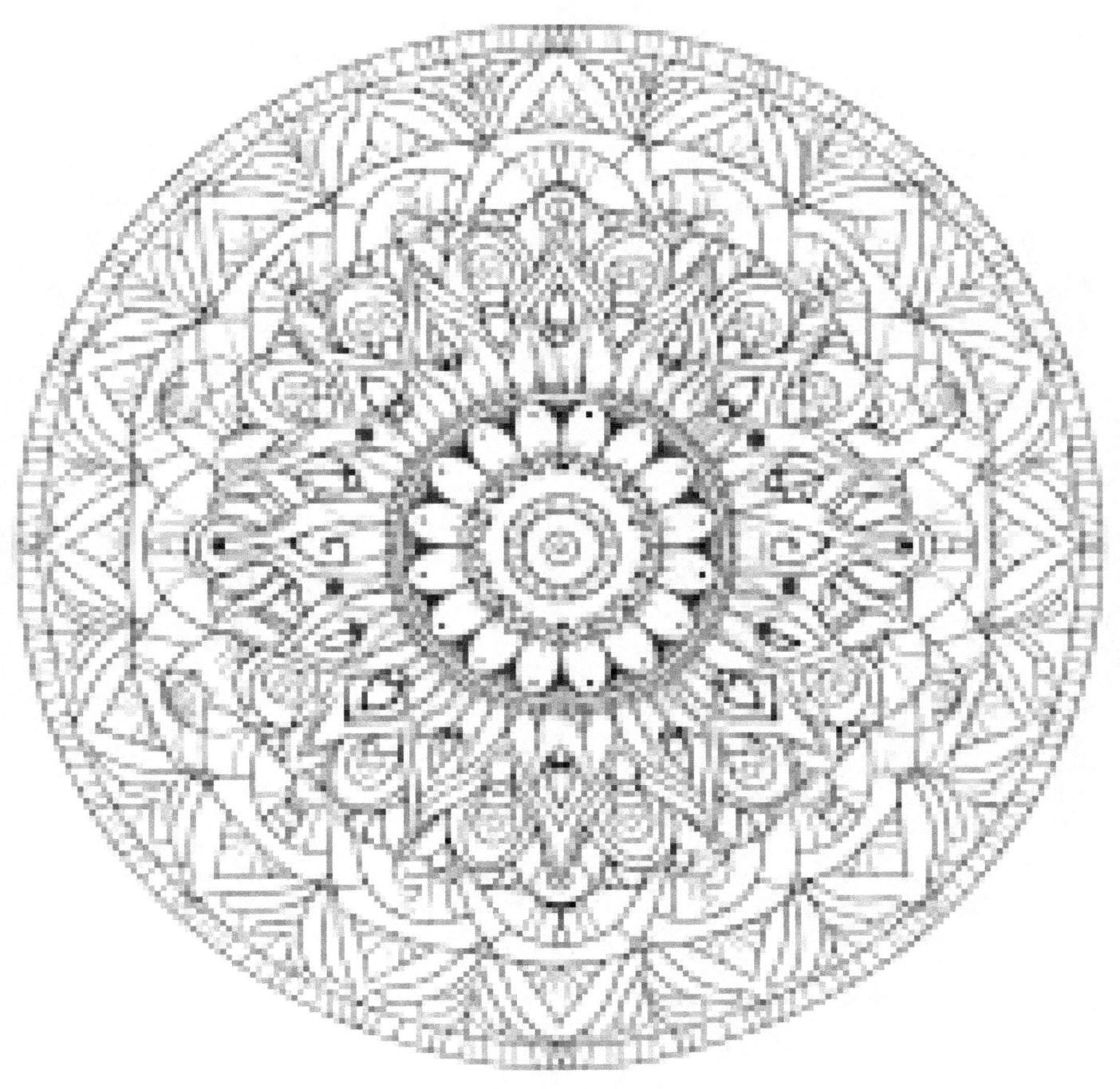

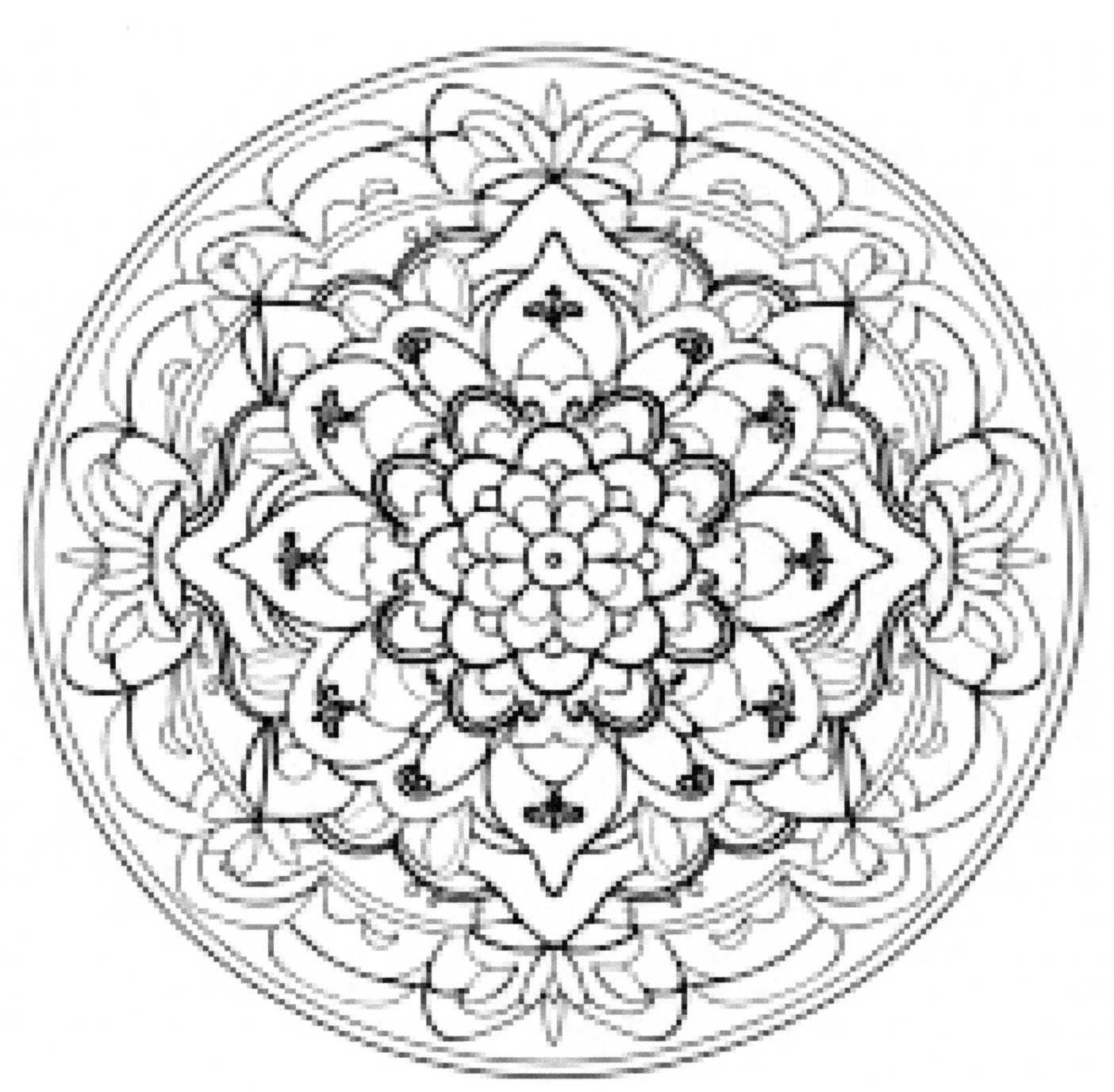

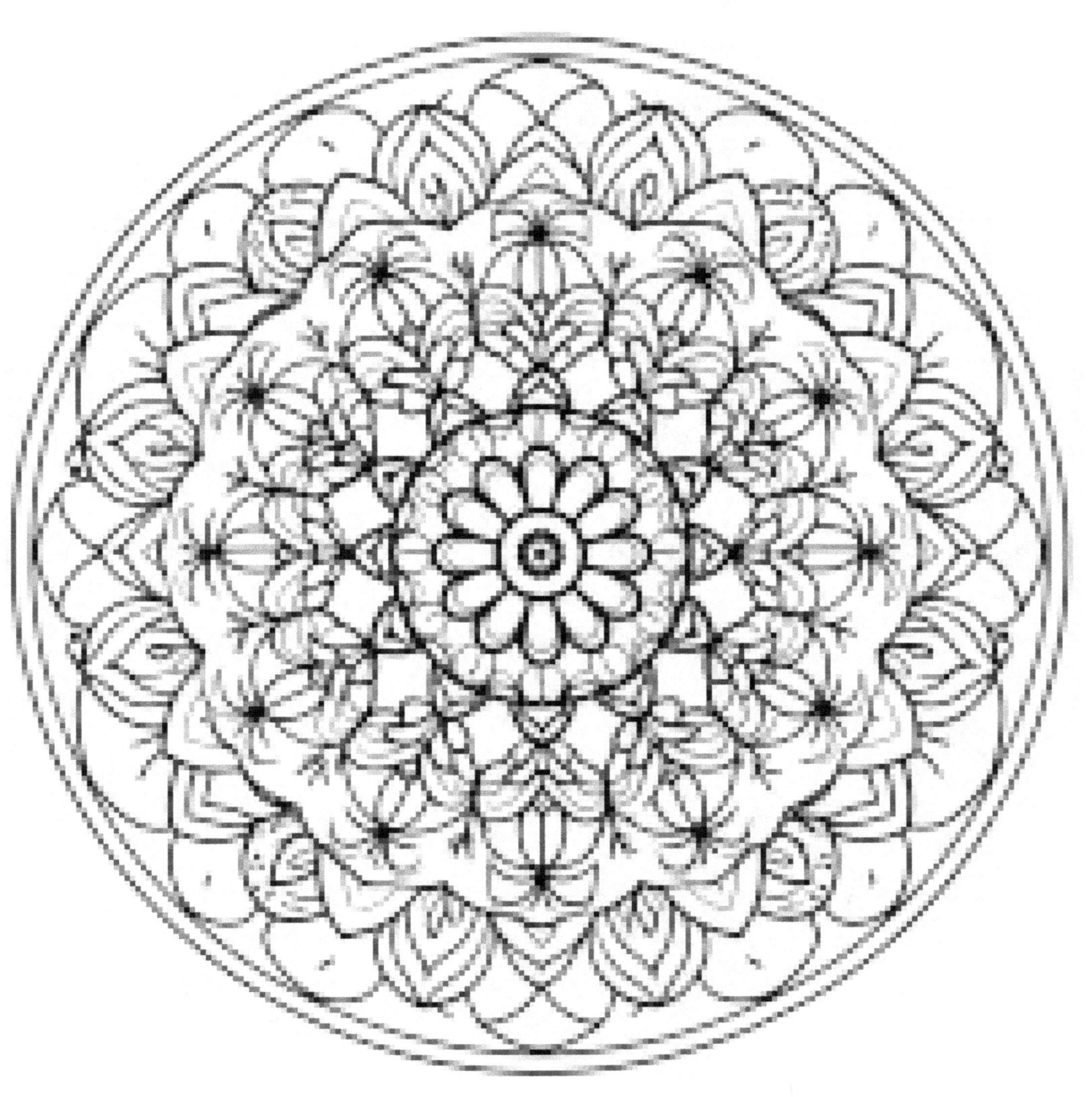

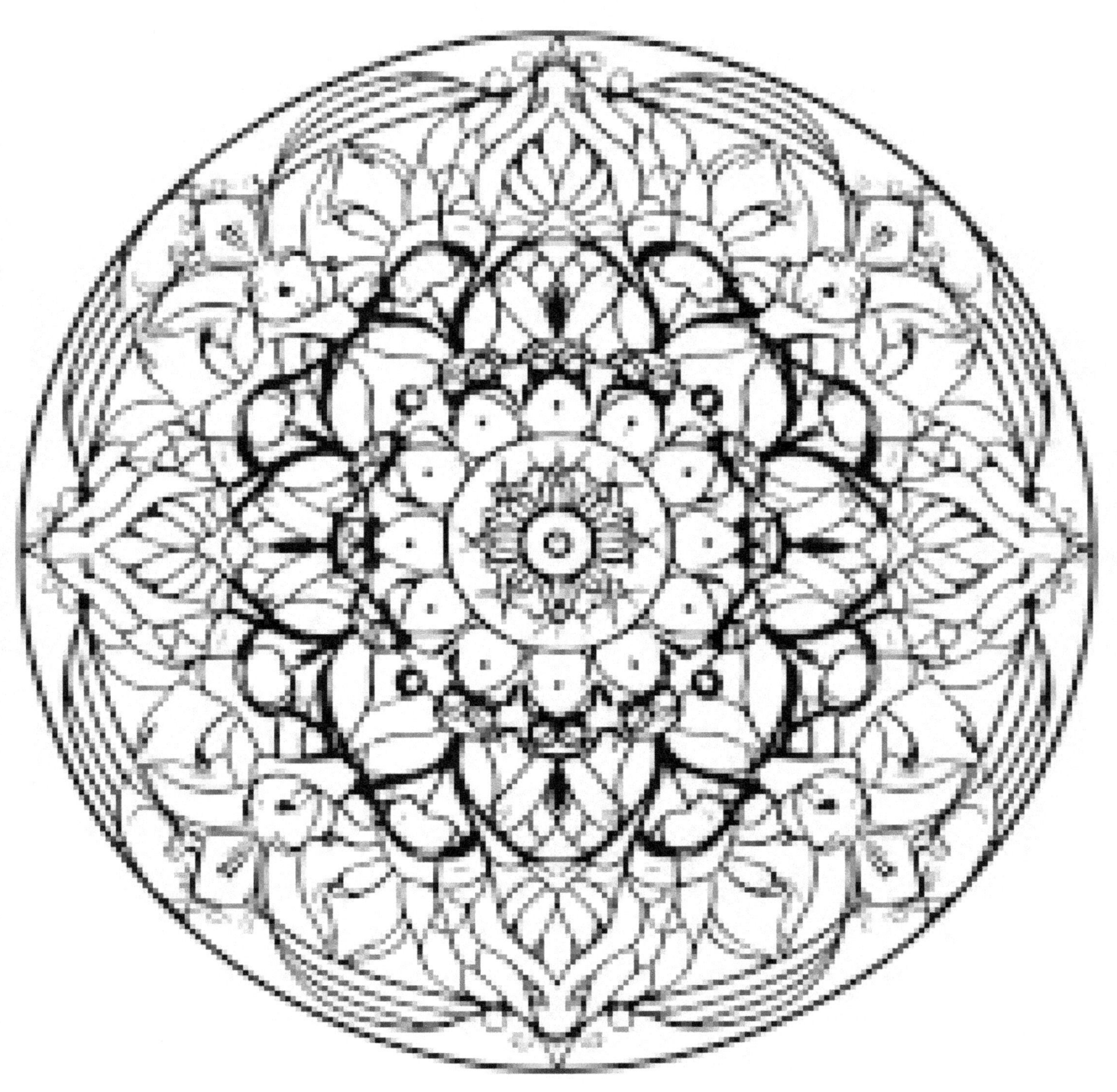

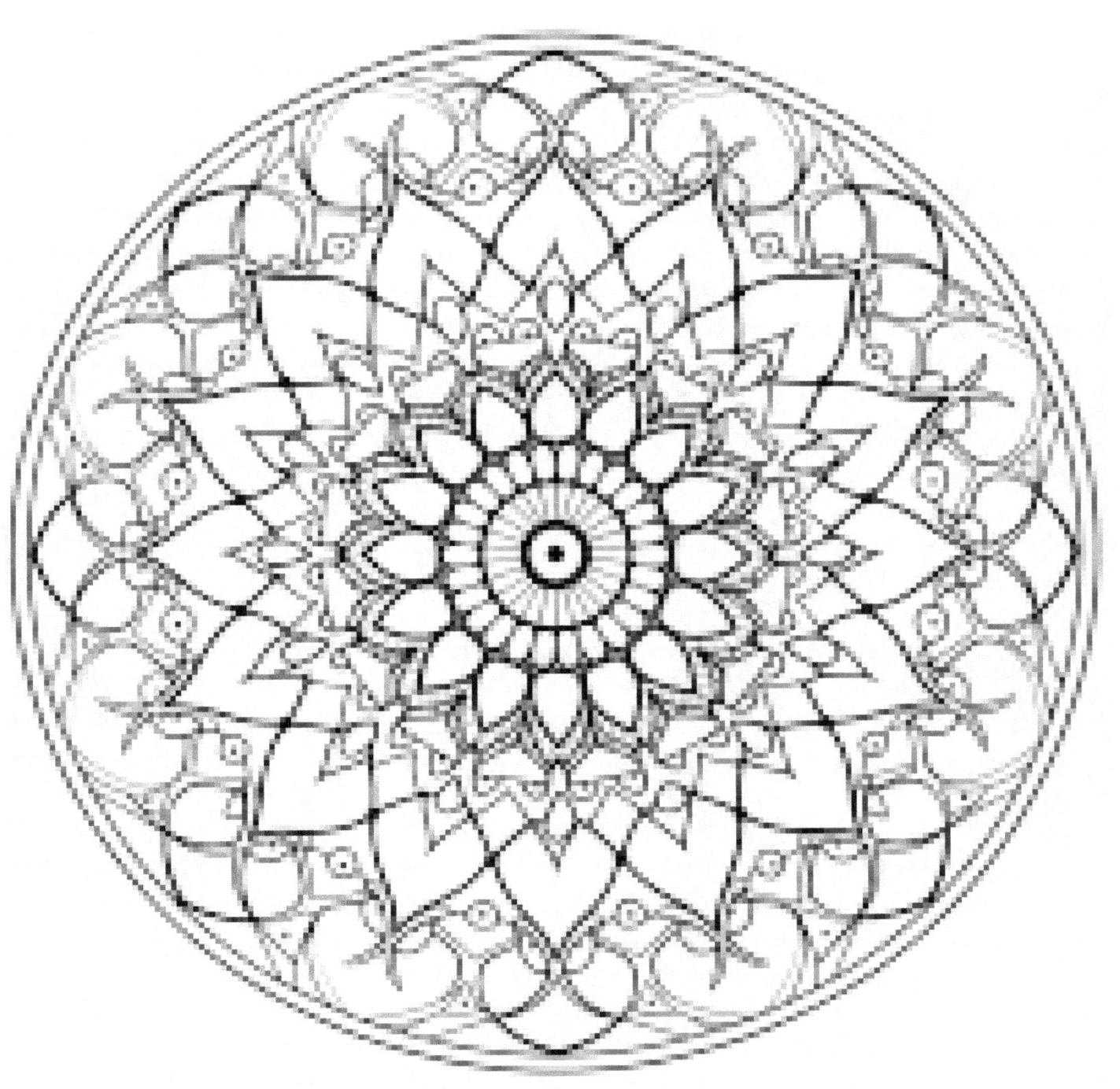

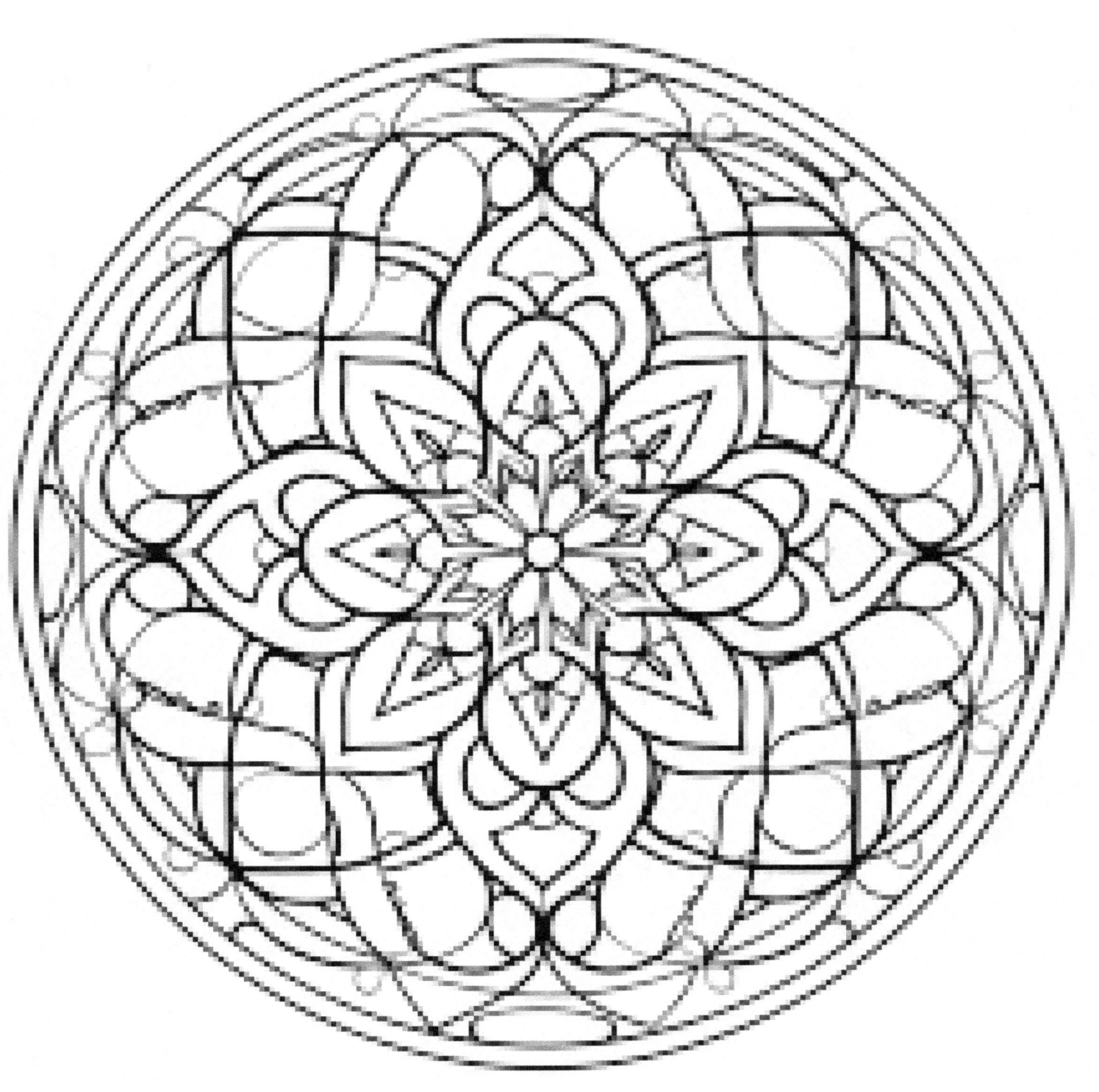

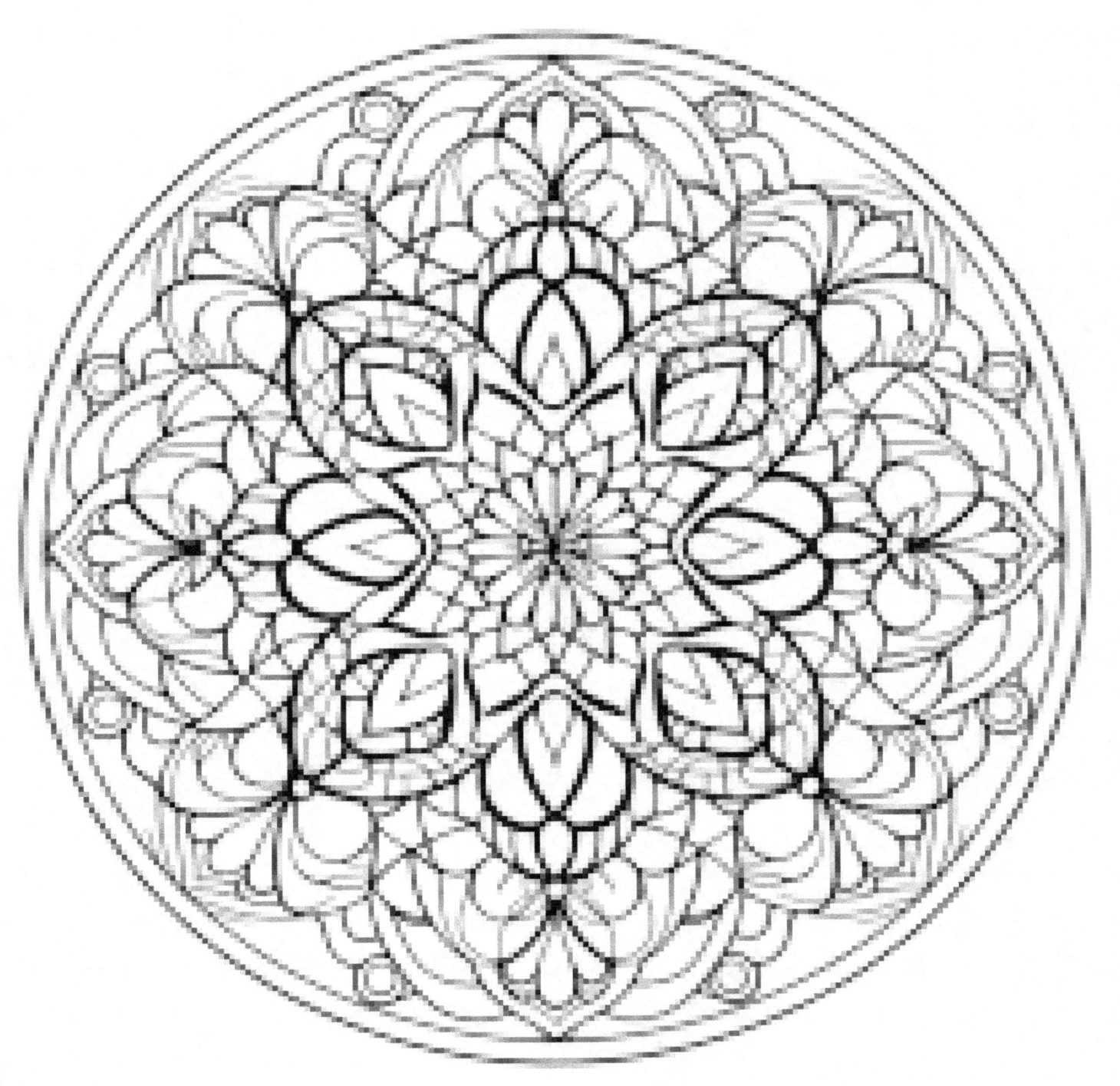

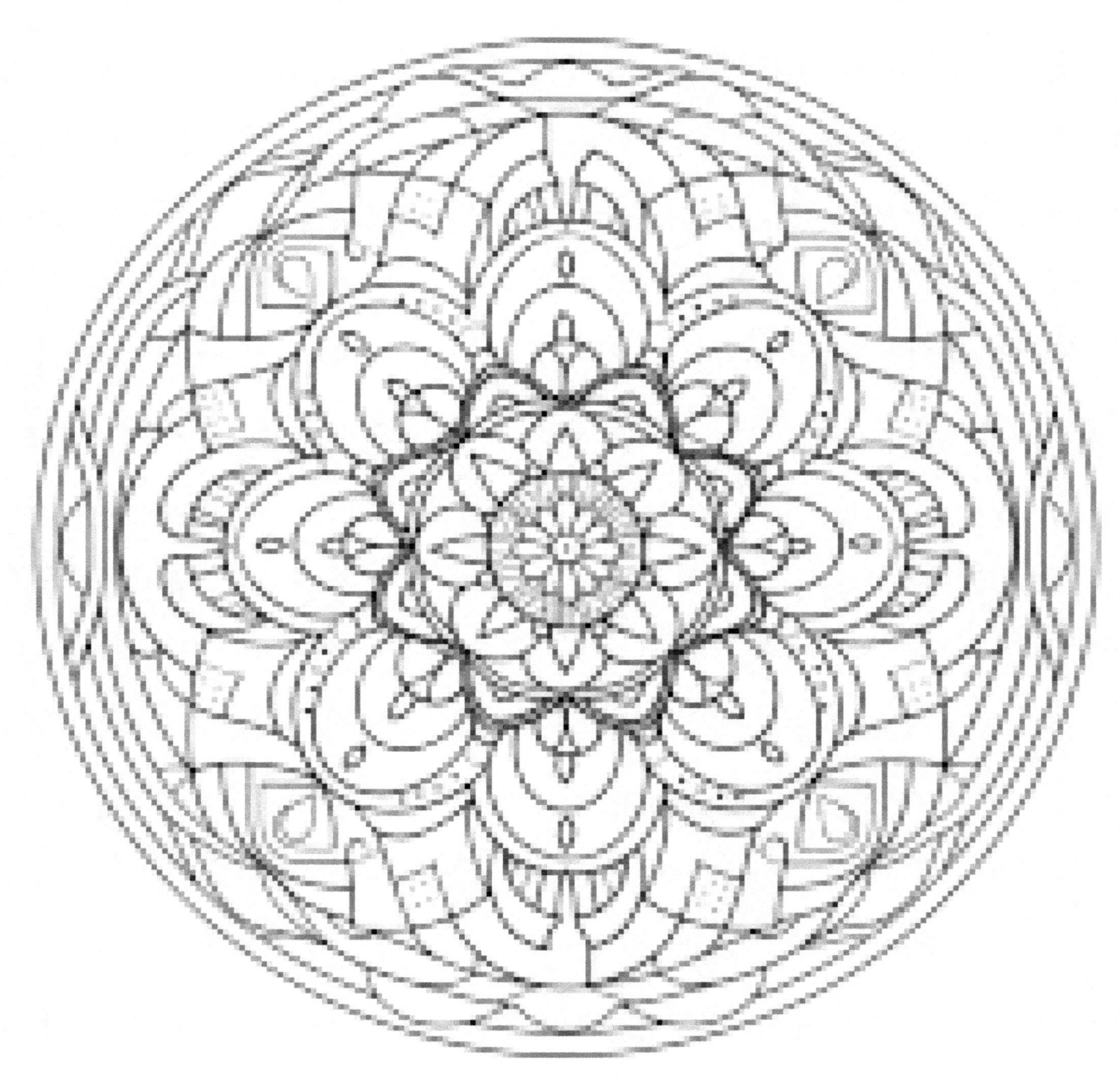

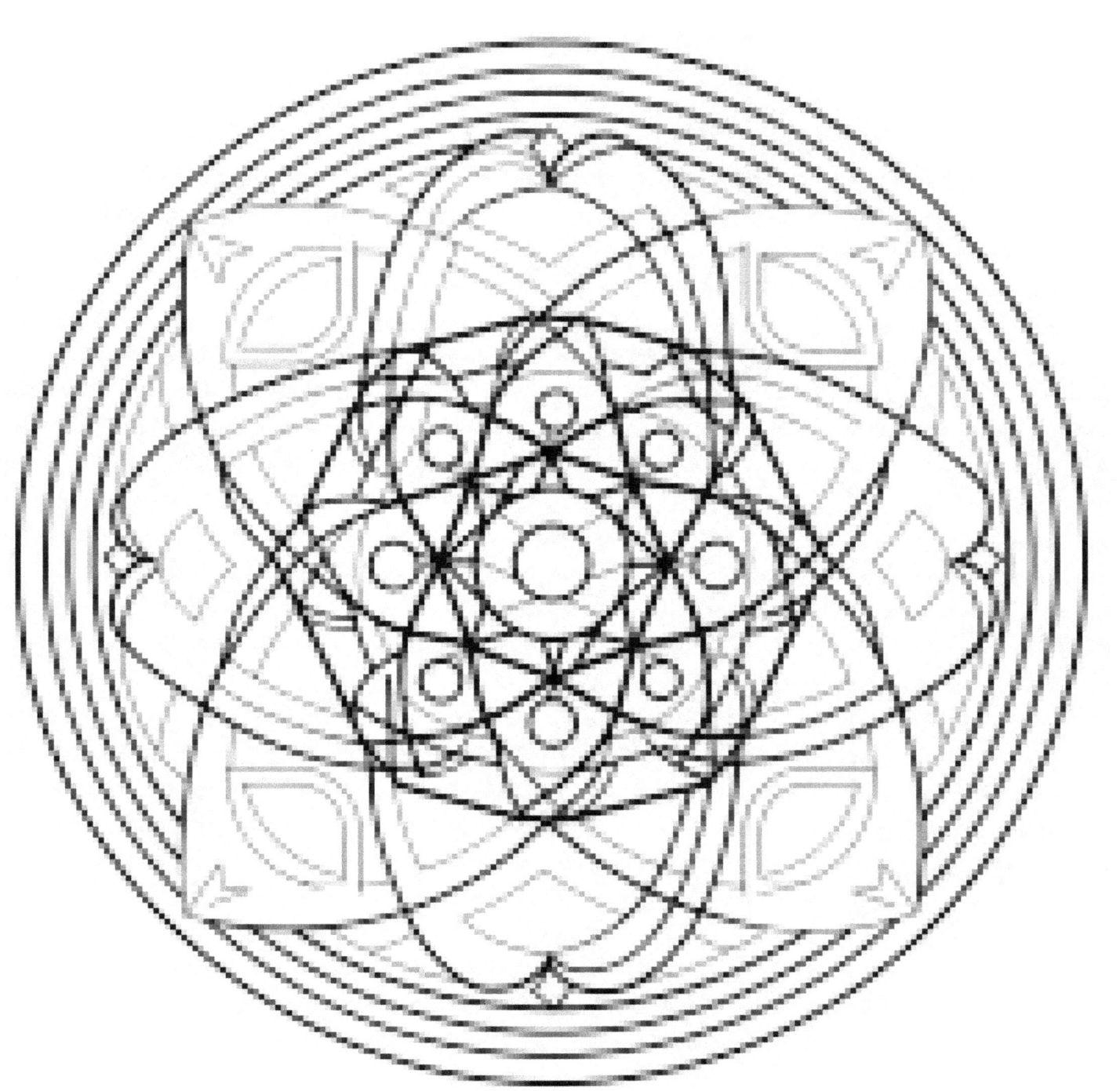

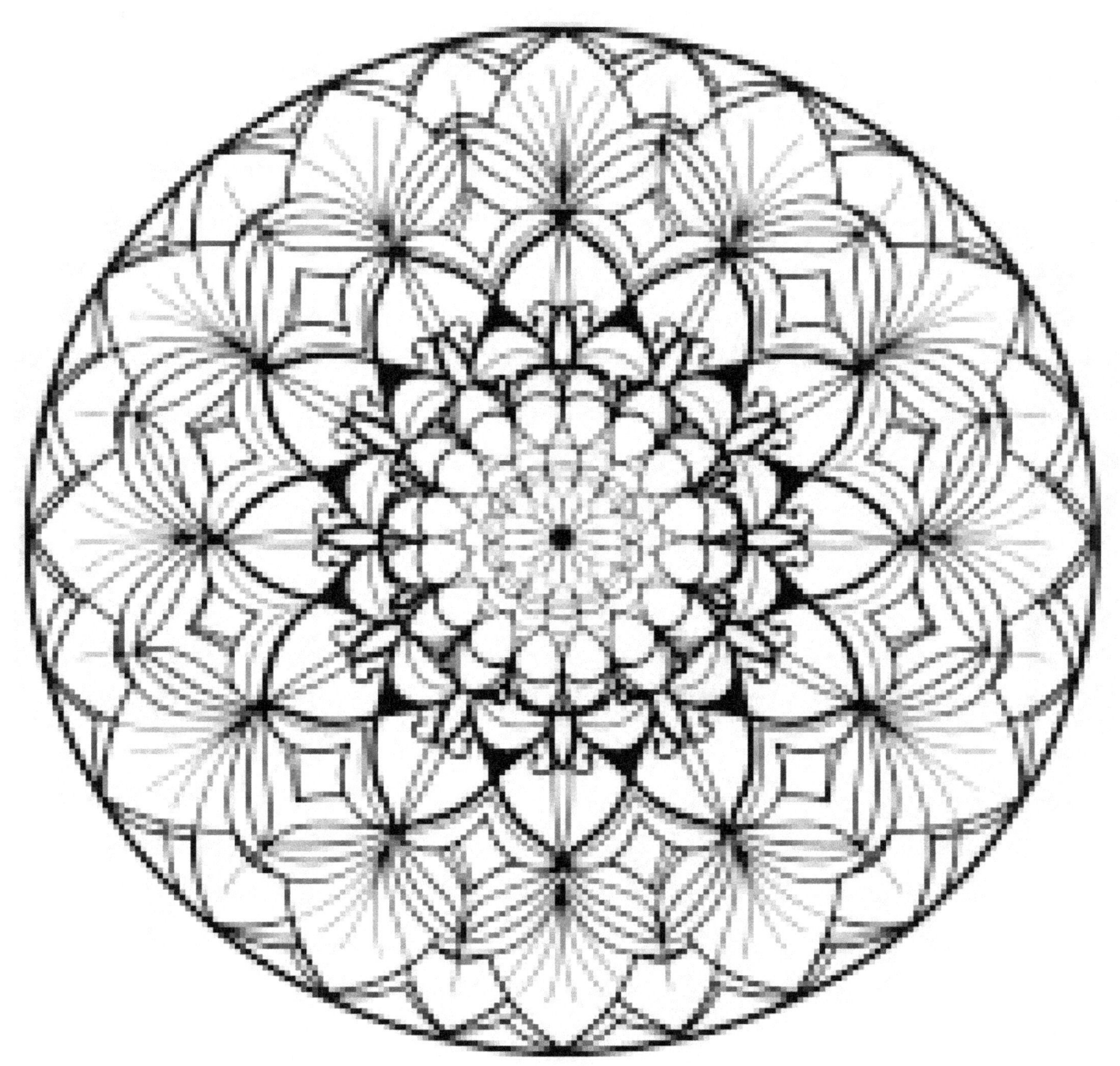

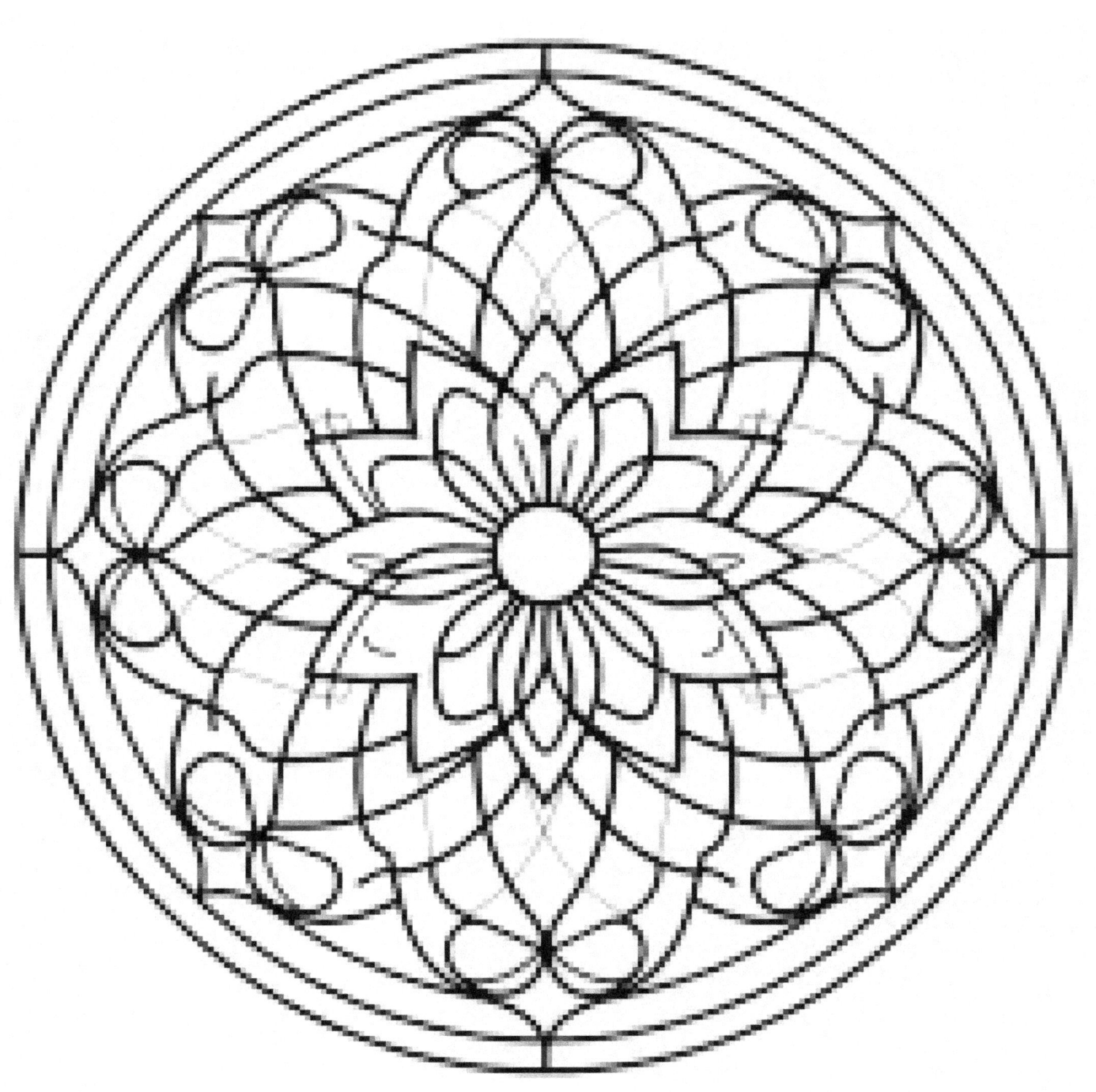

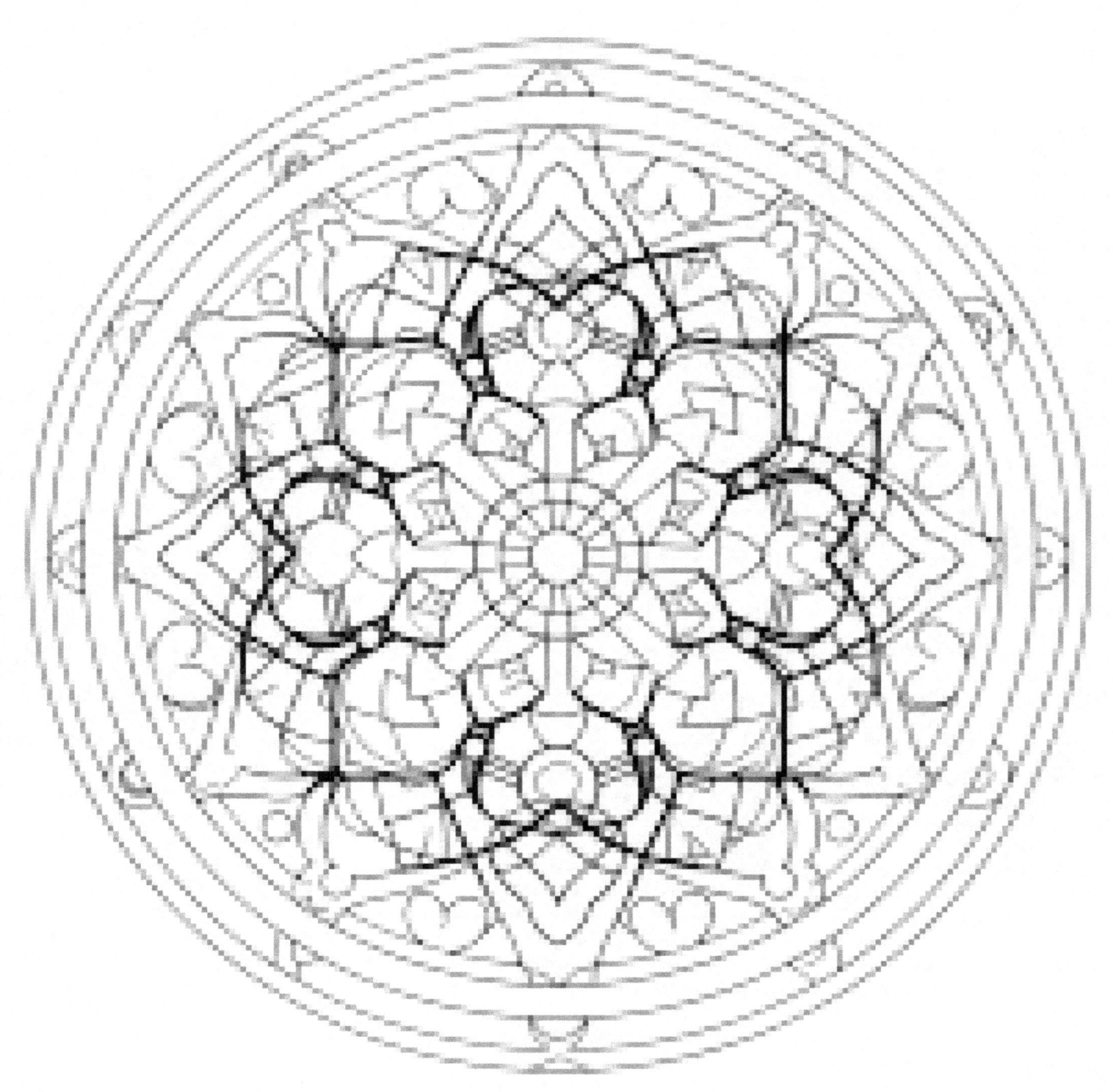

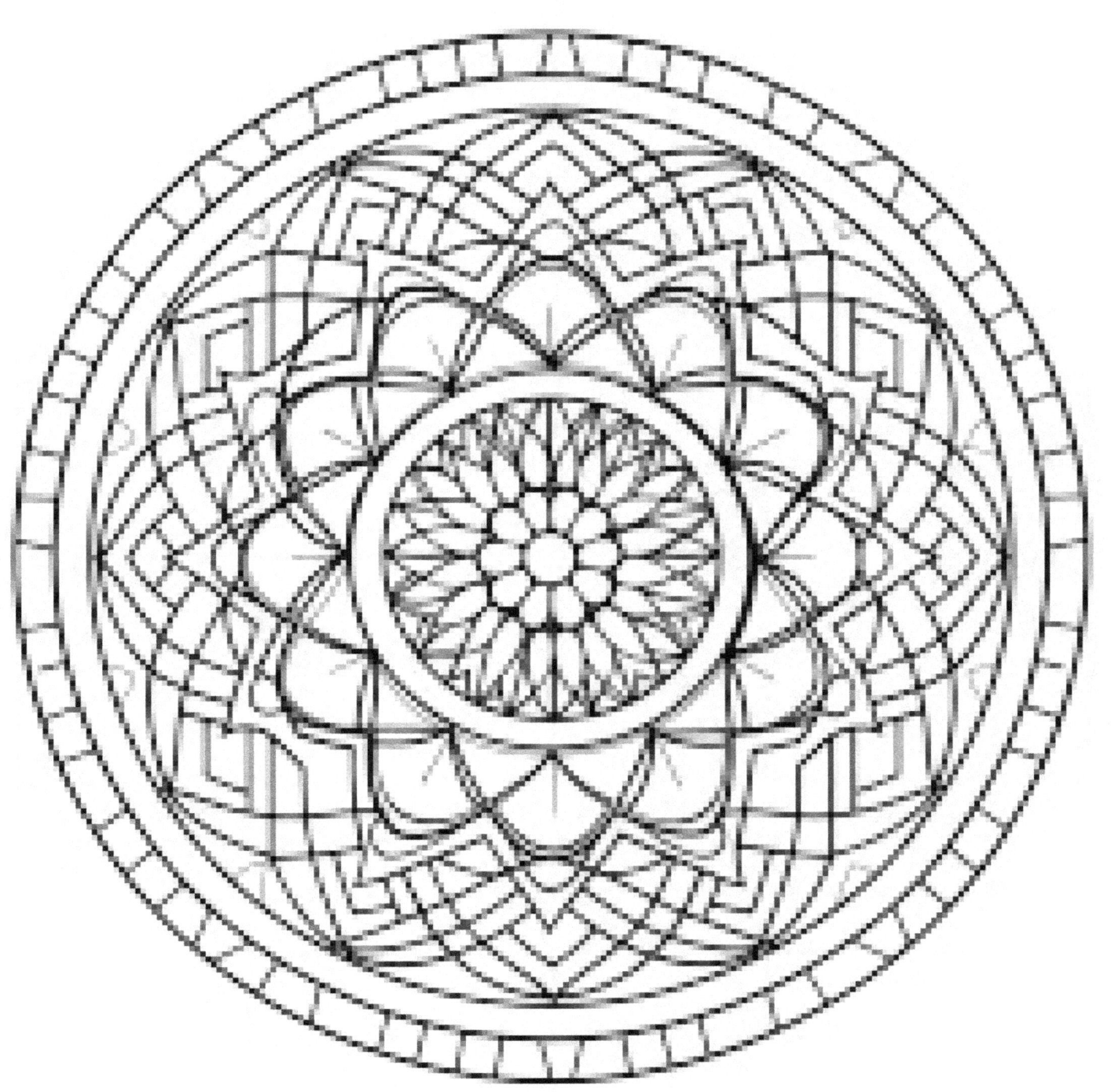

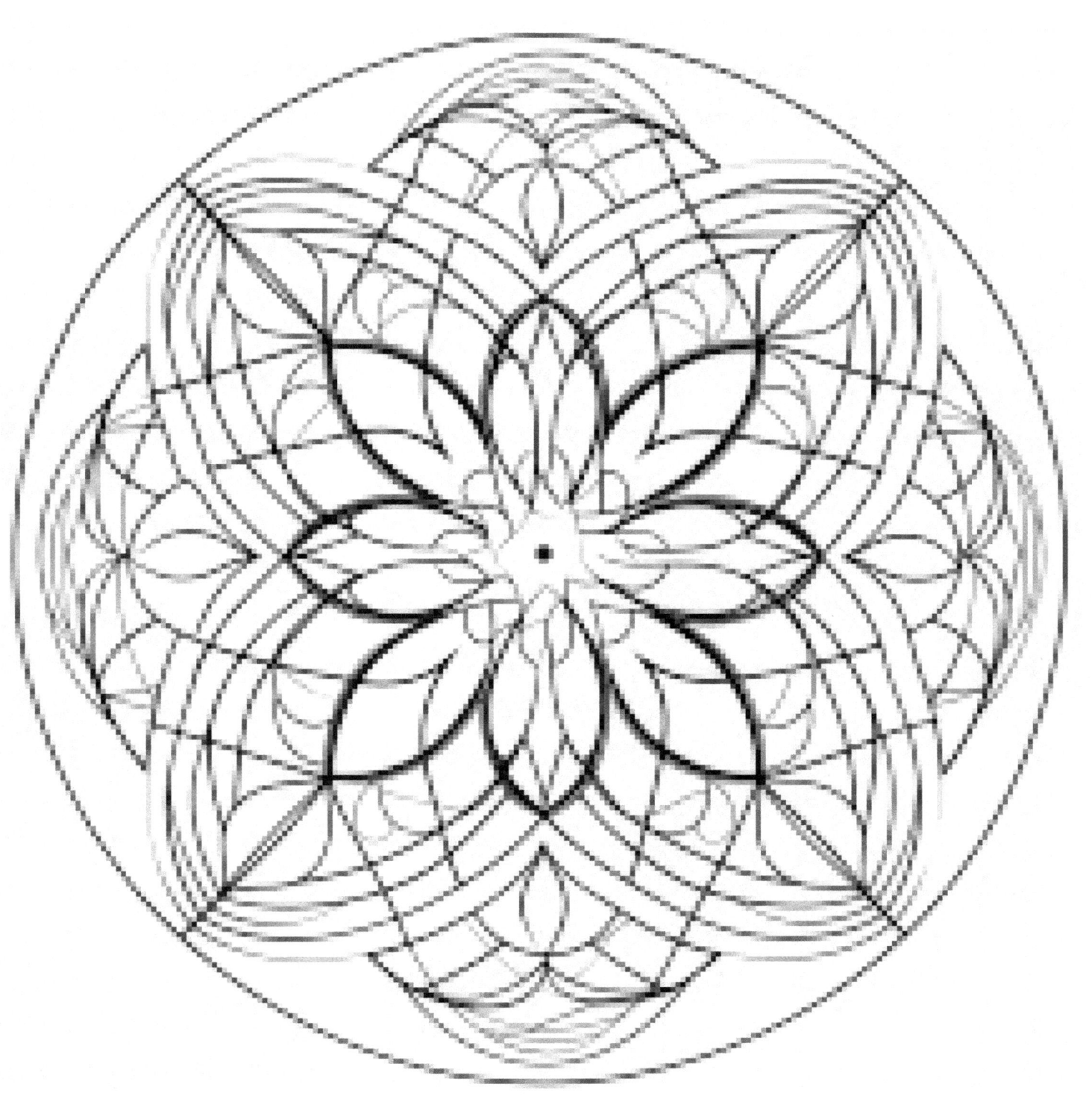

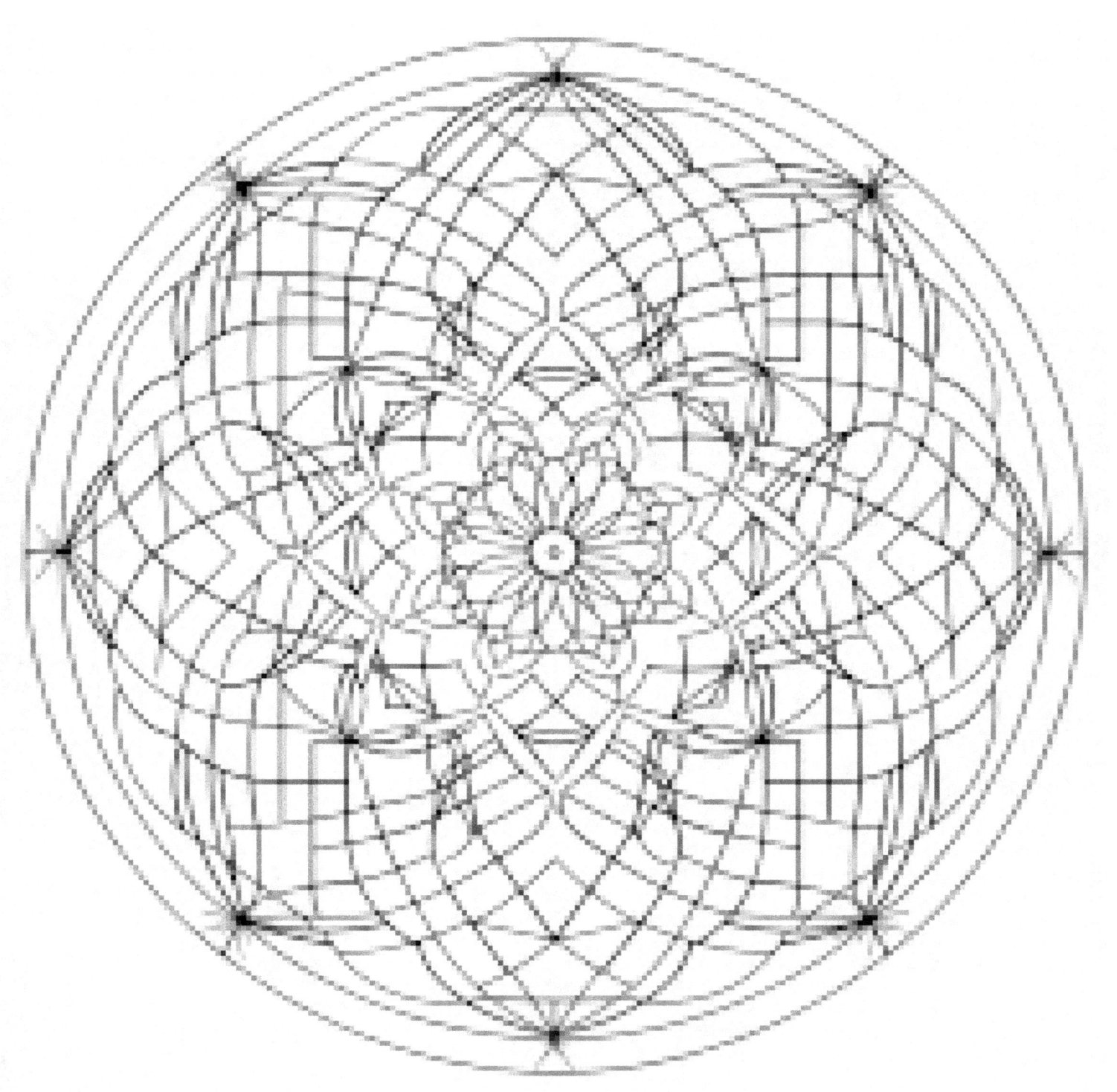

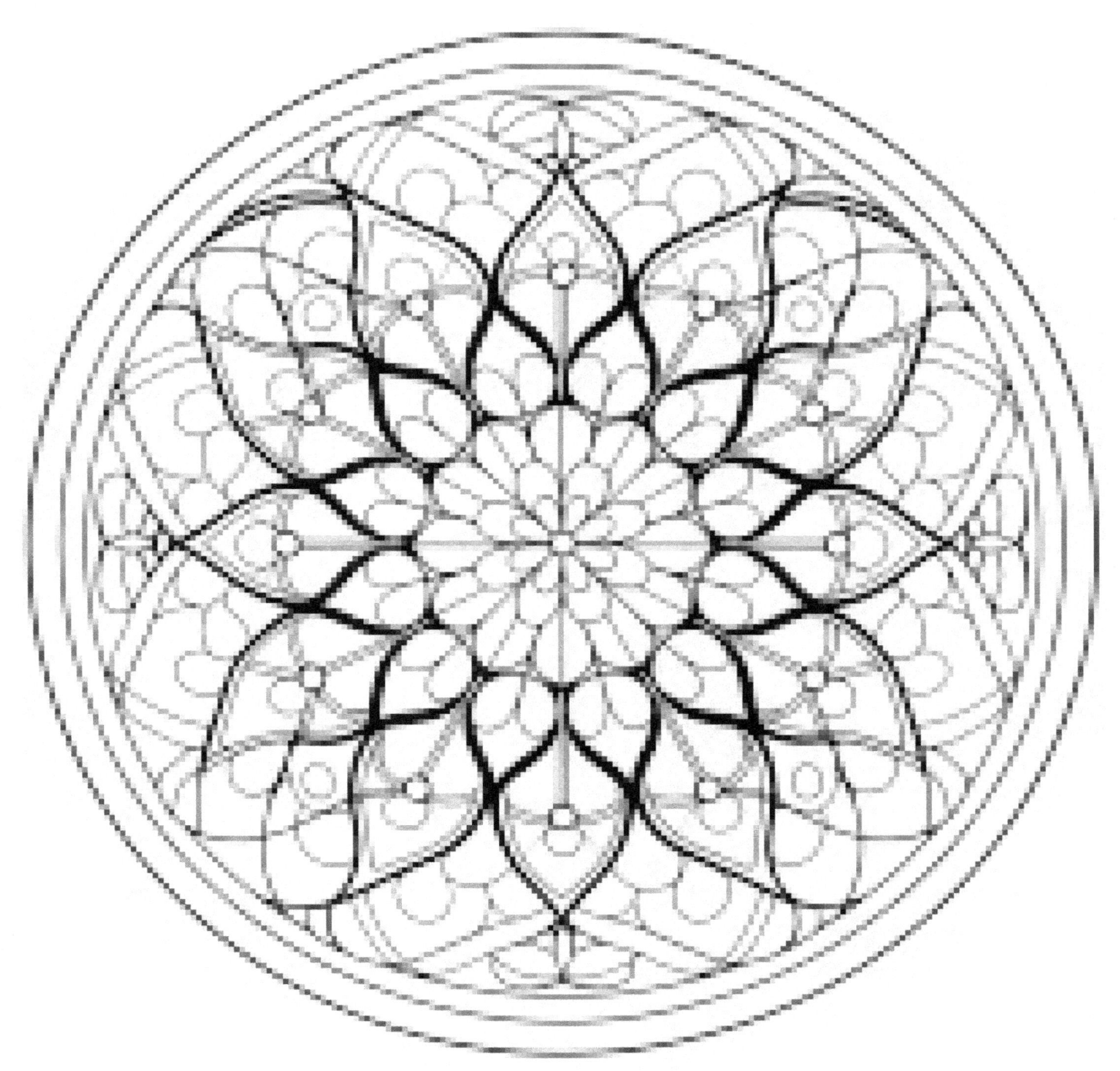

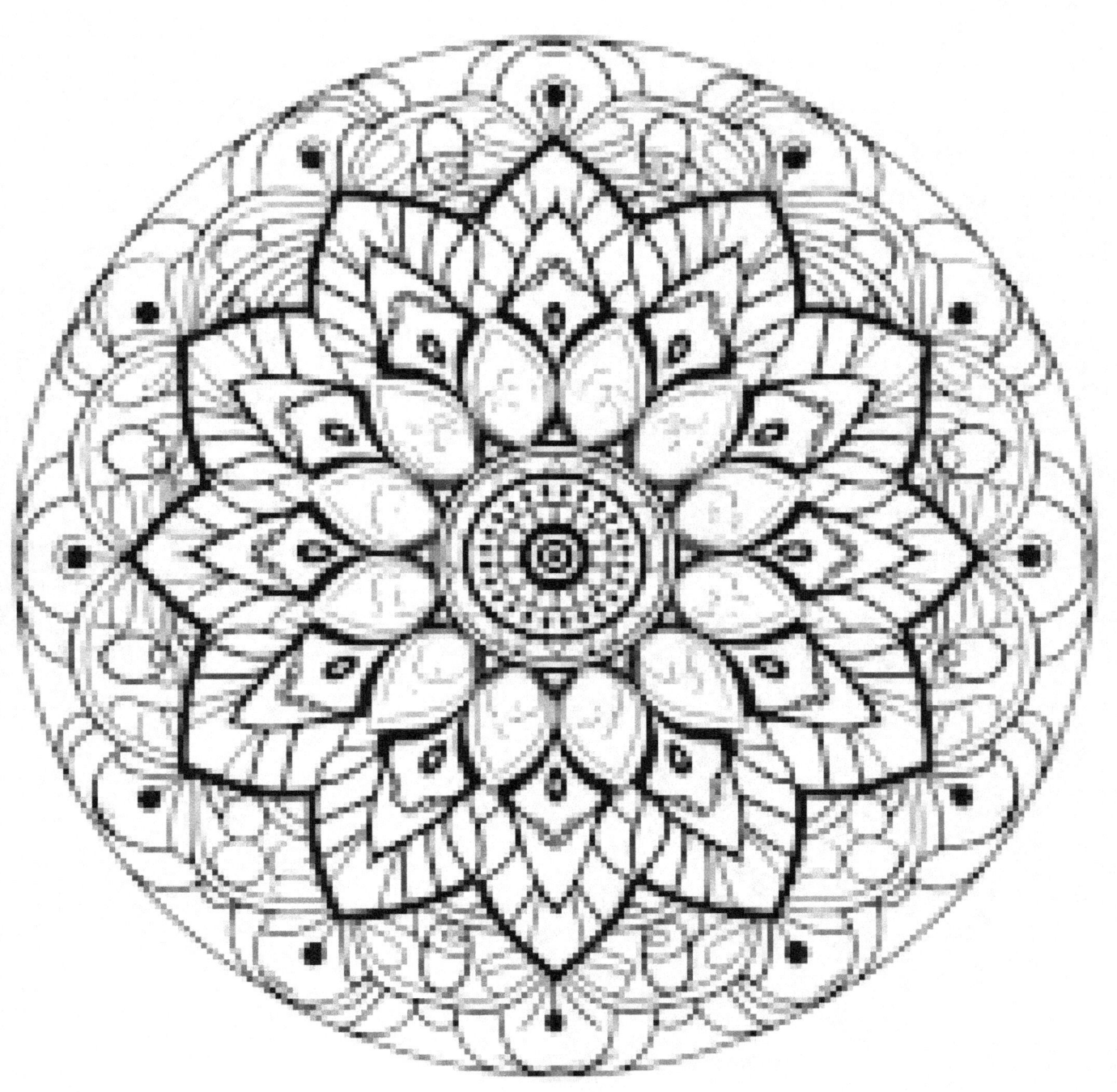

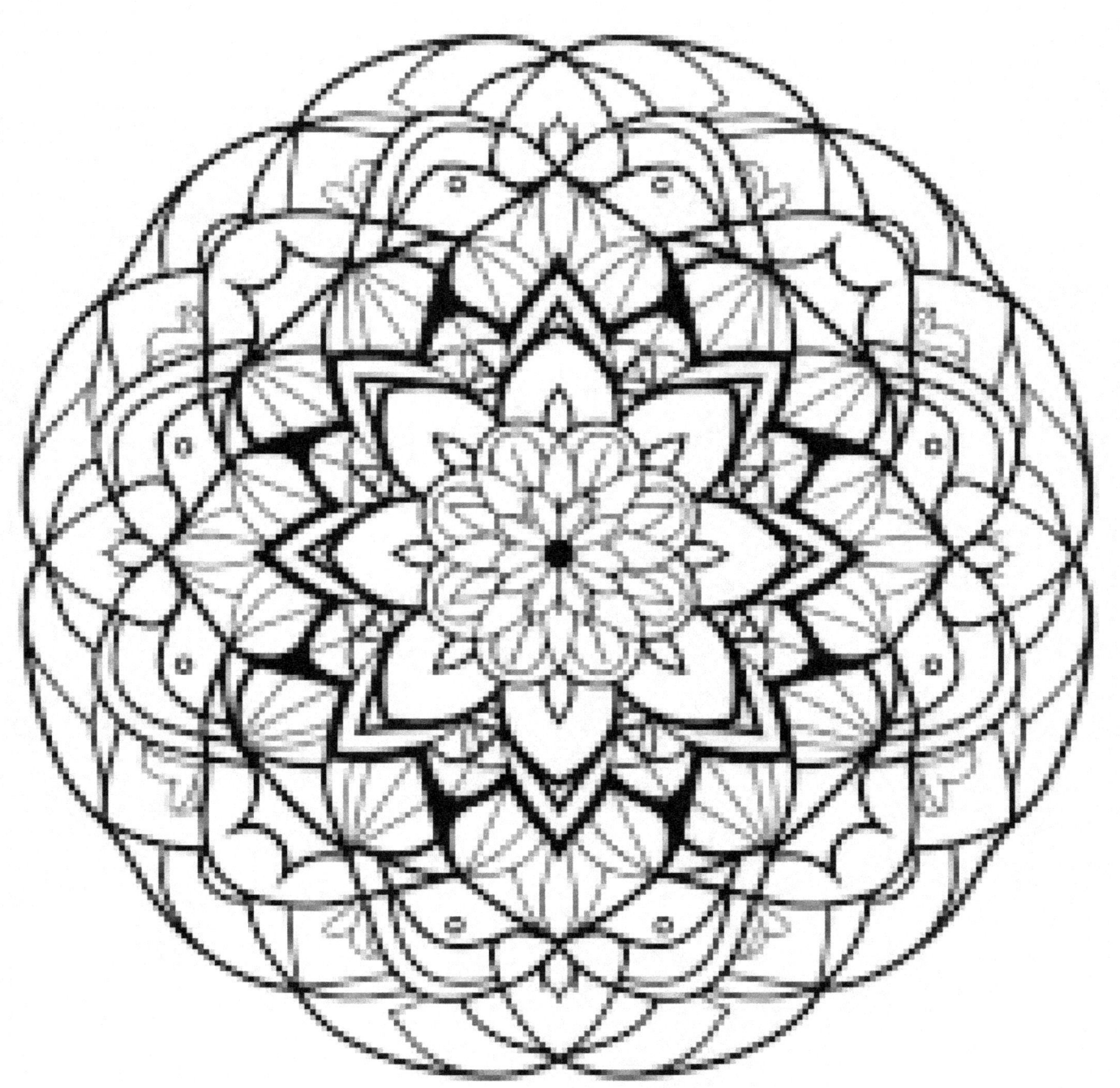

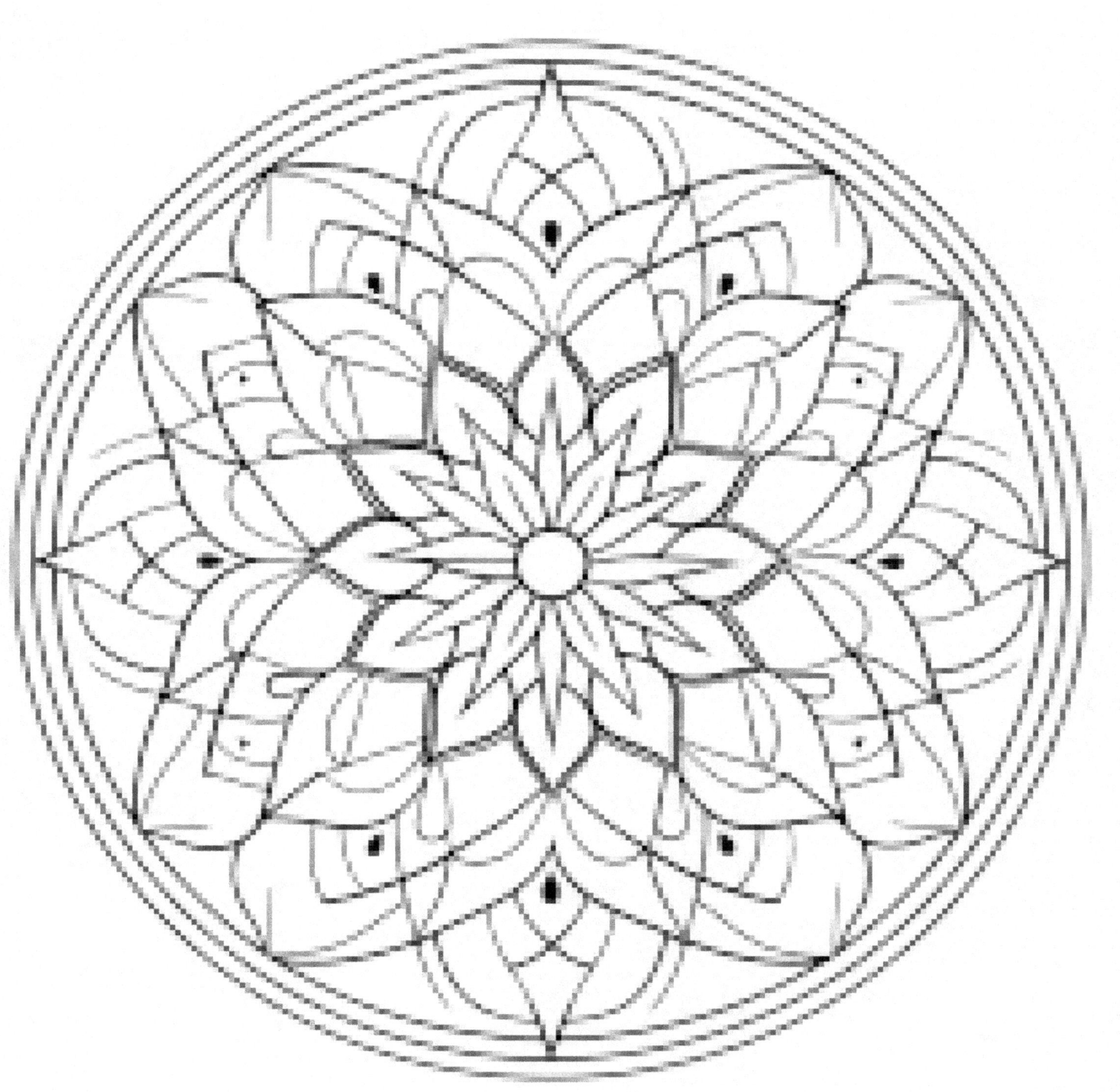

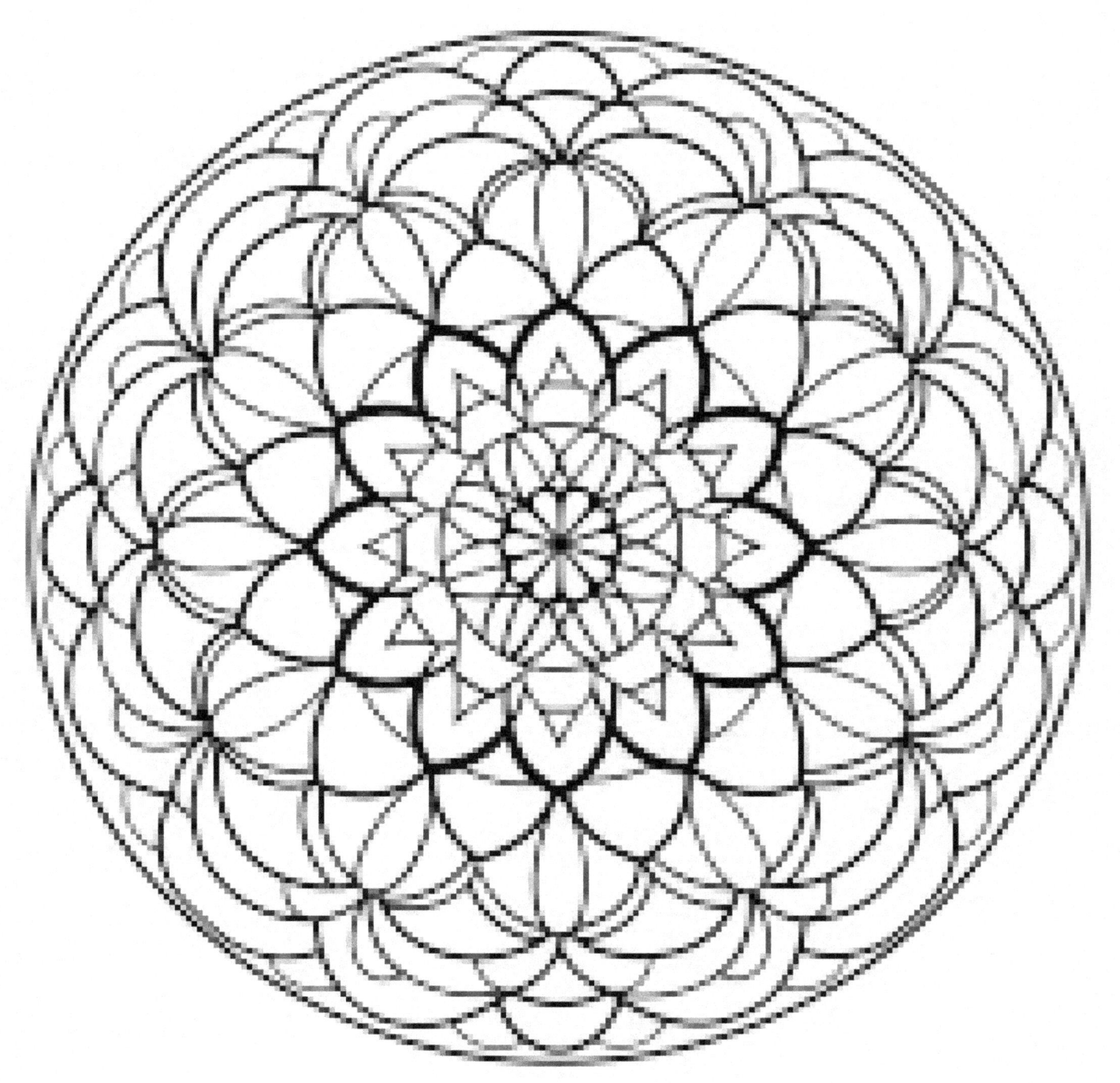

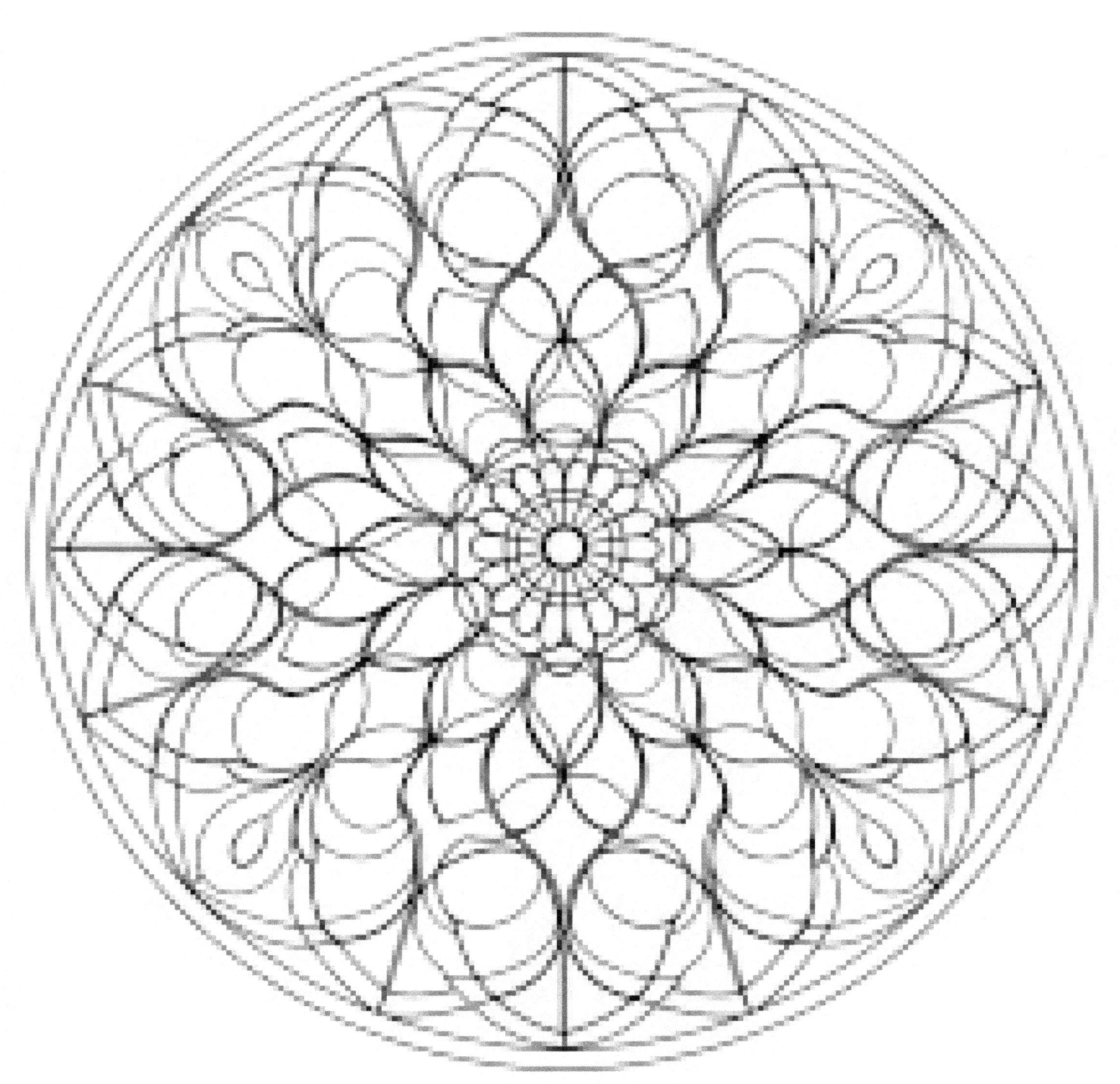

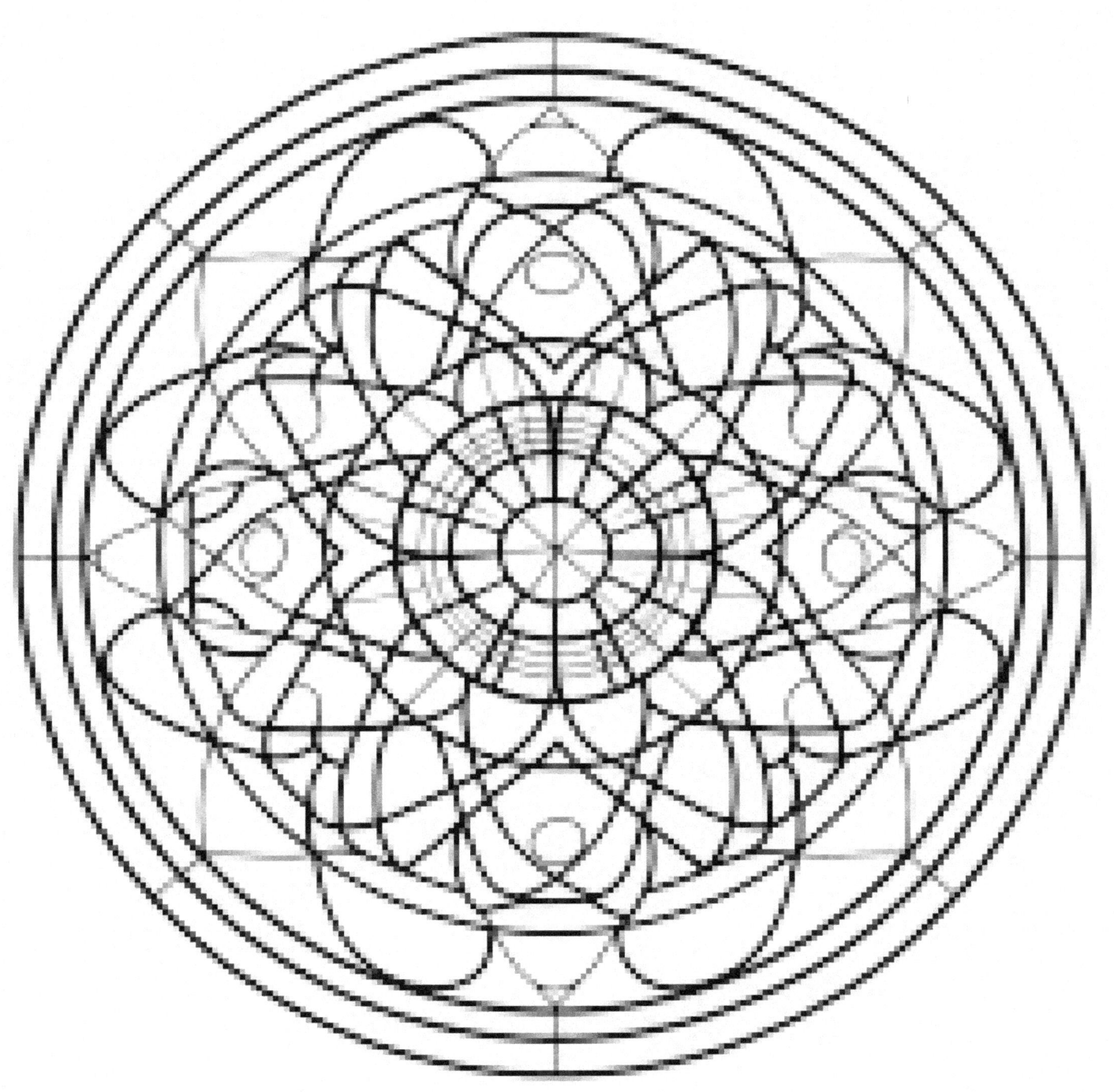

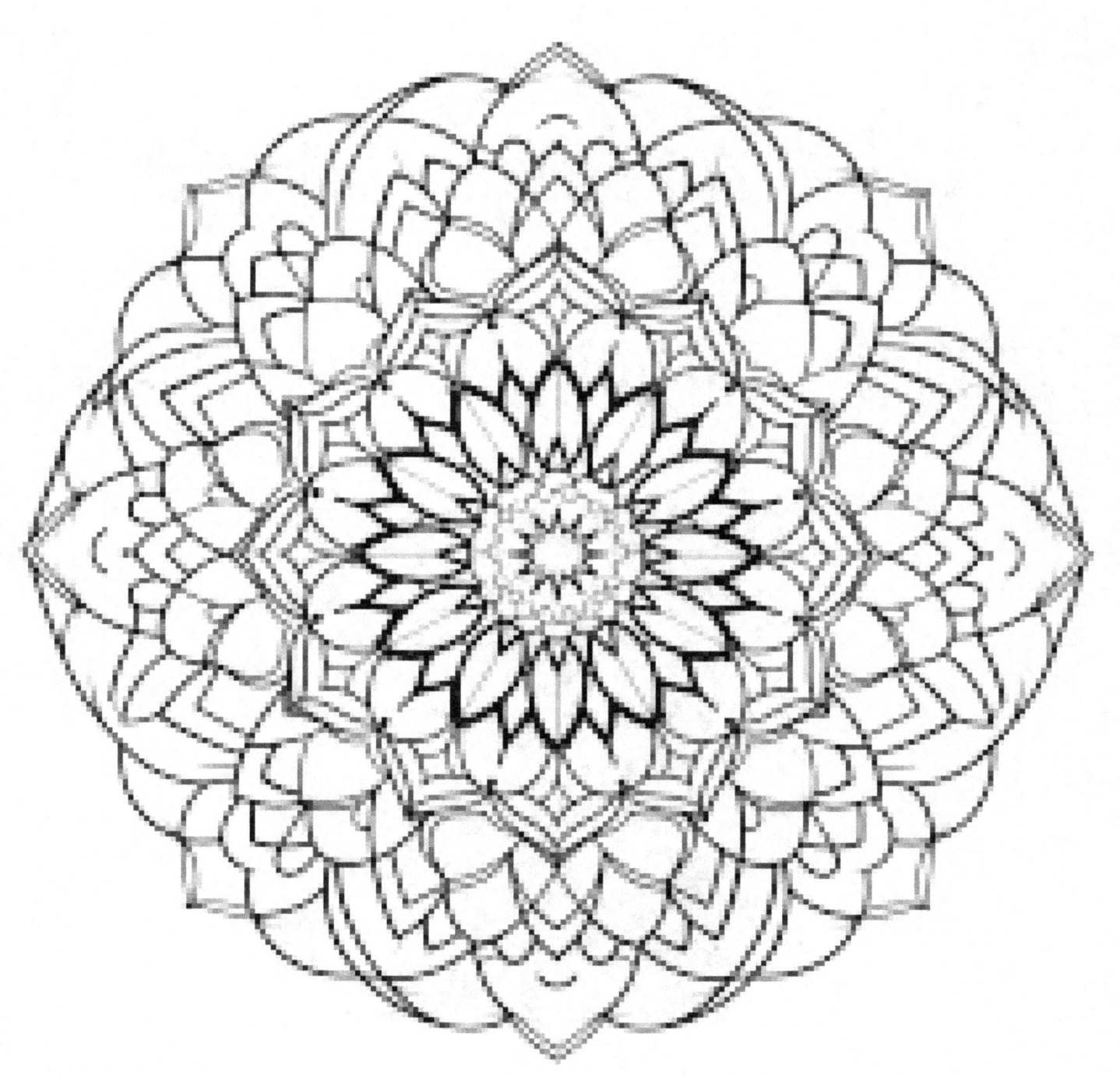

Thank You for Purchasing

Mandala Madness

Visit My Author Page on Amazon

Scan the Above Box Code

www.ingramcontent.com/pod-product-compliance
Lightning Source LLC
Chambersburg PA
CBHW081522220526
45467CB00010B/3010